The D/G Melod

ABSOLUTE BEGI

DAVE MALLINSON

Detailed melodeon tuition designed to speed up the learning process.

Foreword by Andy Cutting

When asked to write the foreword for this book I thought of the occasions that I have met Dave and the great influence he has had on the session scene in England. His enthusiasm for the music and box playing is quite something. He is nearly always the first in a session, guiding the music and, no matter the standard, he always encourages everyone to play their part.

A few years ago, whilst teaching at *Melodeons at Witney*, Dave had to play as part of the concert in front of 150 box players. He was not that comfortable with the idea. So, on stage, he took us on his melodeon playing history. Starting with his first tune learned on the melodeon, he took us through playing various morris styles and ending with some great session tunes. It was never flashy but Mally showed everyone that it is possible to play simply, whilst passing on a great musical tradition.

For your first steps as a box player, I can think of few people better to guide you. And, if you see Mally in a session, a pint would, I'm sure, go down very well.

Andy Cutting
10th July 2002

A soundtrack (DMPCD0202) has been prepared by Mally to accompany this book. The recording is available from traditional music shops or direct from the publishers.

The D/G Melodeon - Absolute Beginners Dave Mallinson

ISBN 1 899512 01 2

A catalogue in print record for this title is available from the British Library.

Acknowledgements

Photography: Mitch France Telephone: 01422 886349
Rear cover photograph of Mally: James Noon at Chameleon Design Telephone: 01484 304545
Cover concept and design: Mitch France Telephone: 01422 886349
Grammatical proof reading: Alistair Russell Telephone: 0113 226 9209
Technical proof reading: Nick Barber Telephone: 01484 544892

Produced and published by **mally.com**
3 East View , Moorside, Cleckheaton, West Yorkshire, BD19 6LD, U.K.
Telephone: +44 (0)1274 876388 Fax: +44 (0)1274 865208
Email: mally@mally.com Web: http://www.mally.com

A mally production

Introduction

The aim of this book is to get students off to the best possible start on the D/G melodeon, by presenting information that might otherwise take years to accumulate. The D/G melodeon is just one of a group of instruments, what may be termed the squeezebox family, which is part of the free reed instrument range.

There are many styles of traditional music where the melodeon and its siblings play a major role. Irish, English, French, Tex-Mex, French Canadian, Cajun, Morris and Xydeco are all typical examples. This is not intended to be a specialist book but it endeavours to give students a good grounding, helping them to easily move on to whatever music genre takes their fancy. However, the lessons within are completely based on traditional playing styles and tunes from Britain and Ireland.

Until recently, in Britain at least, there were very few tuition books on the market for any member of the squeezebox family, and those that were available, did more harm than good. This book is loosely based on a series of books I wrote in 1986 called Mally's Melodeon Methods. It has been completely revised and re-written, based on more up to date knowledge and ideas. It has also been re-typeset using modern techniques.

In all walks of life, whether it be mathematics, designing aeroplanes or playing the violin, mankind progresses by first being taught what previous generations have learned, before moving on. Unfortunately, in the case of the melodeon, this doesn't seem to happen; melodeon students all seem to have to start at rock bottom and work things out for themselves. Although things are improving considerably there is still a long way to go; hopefully, this book will make a useful and effective contribution to rectifying this situation.

If you want to become proficient on any musical instrument, you must practise. There is no way round this. You can have the best tuition in the world, but without practice it is useless. Unfortunately, without guidance, it is very easy for students to find themselves practising unsound techniques and falling into bad habits and sloppy playing. It is the intention of this book to steer players into acquiring efficient techniques and to help them develop good habits, from day one. I have assumed that readers of this tutor have no previous knowledge of the melodeon or music: all topics start with absolute basics.

In this book I will be presenting the ideas and techniques that have slowly trickled in over a period of almost thirty-five years. To have had all the information from the start would have saved countless wasted hours of experimentation. It has been a great stumbling block learning a tune, only to find, at a later date, a far superior approach. After discovering a better approach, I would then re-learn tunes, which for an initial period at least, would lead to infuriating confusion. It's much easier to learn tunes for the first time than it is a second time, incorporating techniques newly gleaned. One of the main objectives of this book, is to reduce the chances of being compelled to learn tunes more than once, to a minimum.

I would venture to say that musicians using this book would be able to reach a reasonable standard in a fraction of the time it took me. However, bear in mind the title, "Absolute Beginners": reaching the end of this book is only the start. Also, don't expect things to happen overnight: learning a musical instrument is a difficult challenge. Difficult it may be, but it's not impossible. When things get tough and you feel as if you're getting nowhere, persevere and practise; you will get through it.

Also, don't let the title fool you; although this book is definitely "Absolute Beginners" at the beginning, it certainly isn't at the end. I wouldn't expect anyone to complete it in under two years and, in truth, five years would be a much more realistic schedule. You will progress rapidly through the early pages but prepare yourself: the last few pages (from My Darling Asleep) will be a long hard slog.

There are many different ways of playing the melodeon. Even sticking rigidly to the methods advocated in this book gives plenty of scope for choice. It is not the intention of this book to lay down hard and fast rules, but to provide information for you to make up your own mind: there are always several ways of playing a tune correctly. My main hope in presenting this information is that you learn tunes in the manner that you will play them for life, thus limiting the tedious task of re-learning them.

I consider it very important that you don't rely on this book alone in your quest for melodeon excellence. Surround yourself with music books and recordings. Listen to as much music as possible, both live and recorded. This is the only way to understand the the intricate rhythm and phrasing of traditional music. I have produced a book called *101 Easy Peasy Tunes*, with an optional soundtrack. I would suggest that you might find this a useful source of extra repertoire.

It is extremely important to note that everything you read in this book comes totally from my head: other musicians may be in total disagreement with my ideas. The lessons and methods in this book are only my ideas, they are not the definitive guide to melodeon playing or the gospel according to Dave Mallinson. Contradict, modify and interpret in your own way the information presented here, then add your own techniques and ideas.

A few months after I acquired my first melodeon I asked an experienced player for some advice, his answer was, "Practise, practise, practise and when you're sick of practising, do some more". Not the answer I was hoping for but it's the best bit of advice I've ever had. Remember this: **The value of this book is directly proportional to the number of hours a day you practise.**

Dave Mallinson
July 2002

The Squeezebox Family

The Squeezebox family of instruments is a section of the free reed range. Instruments not included are concertinas, piano accordions and continental chromatic accordions. Instruments in the squeezebox family all have straight rows of buttons on the right hand side. Different notes sound on the press and draw of the bellows. They can be called melodeons or accordeons. Although it is an incorrect spelling, I like to spell the word accordeon in the French manner, when referring to instruments that sound different notes on the press and draw. I use the correct spelling when referring to accordions that sound the same note on both bellows directions. There can be up to five rows of buttons, but instruments with more than three are rarely seen outside of Austria and don't really concern us. On the left there are usually eight or twelve bass buttons, arranged in two or three squares. Some instruments have the full bass system, consisting of up to one hundred and twenty buttons arranged diagonally, as found on the piano accordion. Some instruments may have one row substantially shorter than the others.

What you call these instruments seems to depend on where you live. In England, they are mostly referred to as melodeons. In Ireland, they are called accordeons, except the one row which is called a melodeon. In the southern states of America, even the one row is called an accordeon.

Whatever you call them, they all have straight rows of buttons, each of which plays a scale (except short rows: the notes found on short rows can be anything, but usually they are notes unavailable elsewhere). The first note of the scale is on the press, the next on the draw, and so on. The relationship of the rows to each other splits these instruments into two distinct groups, diatonic and chromatic. Any particular combination of rows is called a system, for example B/C system. Instruments with one row, and multi rows a fifth apart, such as D/G, are diatonic and I call them melodeons. These instruments don't have all musical notes, unless there is of a short row containing the missing notes. Instruments with scales a semitone apart are chromatic and I call them accordeons. These instruments have all musical notes: all notes not found in one scale occur in the other.

Chromatic Button Accordeons

The most popular of these is the B/C: probably ninety percent of Irish players favour this system. The other system, the C♯/D, comes a poor second, but nevertheless, it is used by quite a significant number of players. The advantage of playing the C♯/D is that tunes fall into or near the natural key of the instrument. The main drawback of the C♯/D is that playing requires a lot of bellows reversals, whereas B/C instruments tend to produce a much smoother flow of notes. Inside row buttons on the B/C can be regarded as being the white notes of the piano, and the outside buttons are the black ones. The bass chords found on these instruments, reflect the keys in which they are played (G, D and A), rather than the keys of the system.

Other systems around are the C/C♯ and the D/D♯. These systems don't really count, as they are always played in the B/C or C♯/D style: that is playing the bulk of the music on the inside row, and crossing to the outside, for notes not occurring on the inside scale, mostly F♯ and C♯on the B/C and C natural on the C♯/D. When these instruments are played the music strays away from standard pitch, usually up one semitone. Irish players often refer to this as playing in E flat, or playing the E flat box.

Diatonic Melodeons

Melodeons have one or more rows. Those with more than one row have scales tuned a fifth apart. G/C, D/G and A/D/G are popular systems. The G/C tends to be favoured in France, the G/C/F around the Texas/Mexico border and one rows are played by the Cajuns in Louisiana. Any combination of scales that are a fifth apart is theoretically possible. I regularly use an E/A, A/D, D/G, G/C and C/F.

The most popular system in England is the D/G, because this is the standard pitch of traditional music in Britain and Ireland. Melodeons are useful in folk bands where singing predominates: different systems can be employed when singers vary the keys (see page 32). The D/G melodeon is the instrument of choice nowadays to accompany morris dancing. It is ideal; fairly light, robust, loud, relatively easy to play in this style, and it accompanies itself. The instrument is also widely used in country dance bands. The D/G box is rarely used to play Irish music, even though, in many ways, it is very well suited.

Hybrid Instruments

A combination of diatonic and chromatic systems is possible by using the scales of C♯/D/G, giving the best of both worlds. This system is increasing in popularity, and is now available off the shelf at specialist outlets.

Music Basics for Squeezers

Printed music is a means of conveying musical messages from one person to another, or from one person to many. It's simply a means of communication. It is very useful, because receivers can accept the information at any pace they choose. Acquiring tunes from recordings can be laborious, especially to the unpractised ear. Some passages are often difficult to make out. No such problem with printed music: the information remains static for as long as necessary; it's clear, precise and can be accurately absorbed.

A melody is a series of sounds of varying pitch and length, each sound is called a note. Printed music uses symbols to represent these notes. The shape tells us how long the note lasts, and its position on a grid of five parallel lines and four spaces, denotes the pitch. This grid is called the stave, and each line and space has a name, which is given to any note placed there.

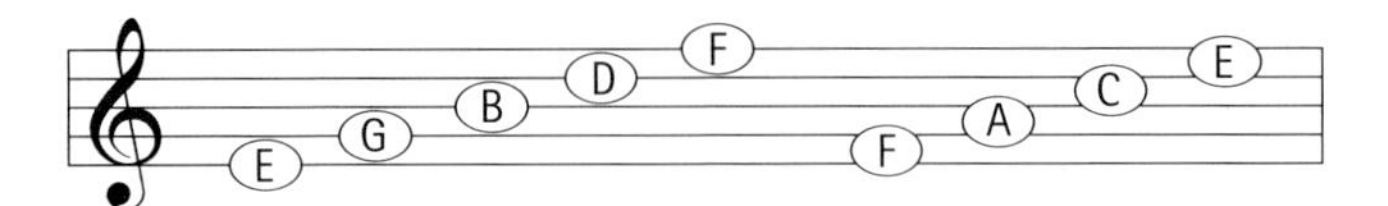

Notes are written on the lines and spaces, and also above and below the stave on small lines, called leger lines. They are named after the first seven letters of the alphabet: when you get to G you start again at A. The symbol found at the beginning of each line of music is called a treble clef. It tells us that the names of the notes are as shown above. You only need to remember one to be able to find out the rest and, just to make it really simple, the notes in the spaces just happen to spell the word FACE, going from bottom to top.

Music for the melodeon always has a treble clef sign at the beginning of each line and, with rare exceptions, a key signature consisting of one or two sharps. A sharp is represented by the symbol ♯; it raises the pitch of a note by one semitone, the smallest interval of musical pitch. When there is one sharp in the key signature, it is always placed on the F line. This tells us that all F notes have to be raised by one semitone to F sharp (F♯). One sharp indicates the key of G major. Here are the main notes of G major.

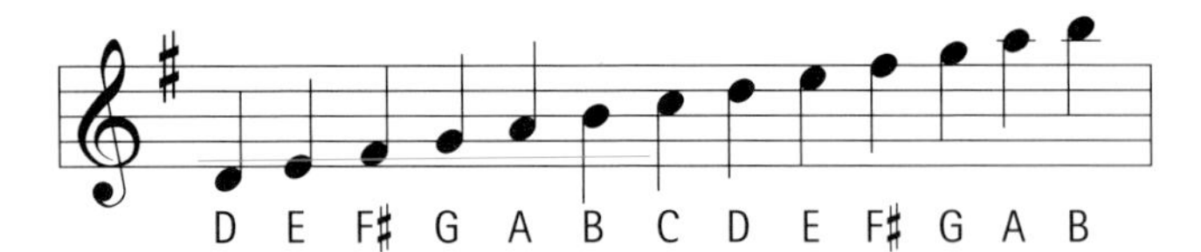

When a second sharp is added it is placed on the C space, so now all F notes and C notes are raised by one semitone to F♯ and C♯. Two sharps indicates the key of D major. These are the main notes of D major.

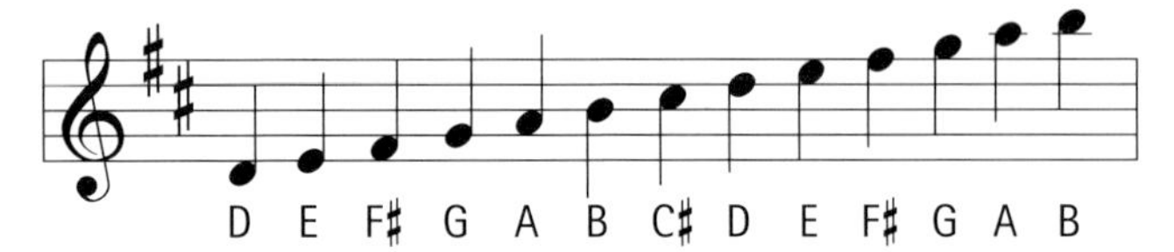

It is important to memorise where to find these notes on your instrument.

The shape of musical notes tell us how long they are to be sounded. The length of time a note is sounded is not an exact measurement of time, but a comparative amount of time in relation to the other notes. Here's how they relate.

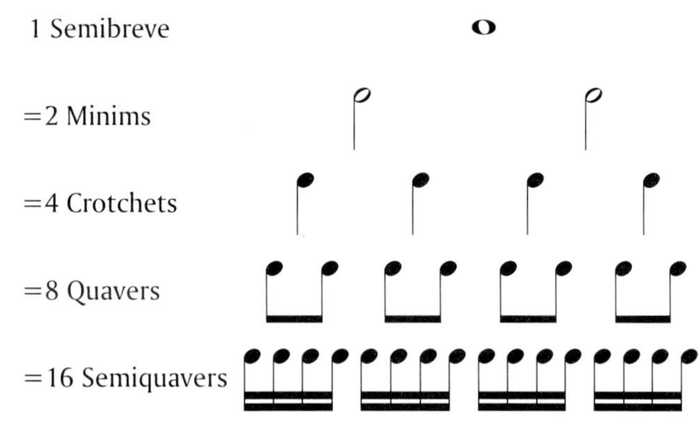

Quavers and semiquavers have the symbols ♪ and 𝅘𝅥𝅯 when they occur singly, but are joined together when they occur in groups. For each note there is an equivalent symbol to indicate a period of silence. These symbols are called rests. Sometimes, a note or a rest has a dot after it, this means that the note or rest is held for half as long again. Rests and their equivalent notes are shown below.

Music has a steady throb or pulse which you can clap along to. These pulses are called beats, some of which are stronger than others. The strong or accented beats occur at regular intervals, forming the beats into groups of two, three or four. A piece of music is naturally divided into equal measures by these groups of beats, which are known as bars. In order to show where these divisions come, bar lines are placed across the stave, in front of the accented notes. Each beat of a bar receives one count. In order to denote what type of beat grouping will present itself in a piece of music, a time signature is placed immediately after the key signature, at the beginning of the piece. The top number denotes the number of counts per bar. The bottom number denotes the type of note that receives one count. Thus:

$\frac{2}{4}$ means 2 crotchets to the bar
$\frac{4}{4}$ means 4 crotchets to the bar
$\frac{3}{4}$ means 3 crotchets to the bar
$\frac{6}{8}$ means 6 quavers to the bar

The symbol :‖ means repeat from the symbol ‖: or if that symbol doesn't occur, repeat from the beginning.

This curved line ♩‿♩ joining two notes of the same pitch together is called a tie; it means the values of the two notes are added together and sounded as one.

The flat ♭ lowers a note by one semitone in pitch.

The natural ♮ restores a note to its original pitch.

|1. |2. Where these brackets occur, play the notes under *1.* first time and the notes under *2.* on the repeat.

Introducing the D/G Melodeon

So you've just acquired your first melodeon. Let's see if we can make some sense of it: it's not difficult. Unlike many instruments, it's not necessary to practise for hours just to make a nice sound. Instruments such as trumpet, flute and violin require hours of work, just to acquire the skill to blow or bow a note correctly. With instruments such as guitar and banjo, you have the irksome task of tuning before you start. Melodeon players are off to a flying start; just press, squeeze and play.

Take a look at your instrument; you will notice that it consists of a set of bellows with a group of buttons on either side. Most likely, twenty-one or twenty three treble buttons are arranged in two vertical rows on one side, and eight bass buttons on the other side. Just round the corner from the bass buttons, you will find an air button. The treble buttons are for playing the melody with the fingers of the right hand. Simultaneously, the left hand fingers tap out a simple accompaniment on the bass buttons, whilst the thumb works the air button. You're a one man band!

Pick up your instrument, press the air button and draw in some air. Press any treble button and squeeze the bellows, you have just produced you first note, easy. Now press several buttons on the same row, squeeze the bellows inward, you have just produced your first chord. Squeezing the bellows inward is referred to as the press of the bellows; pulling the bellows out is called the draw of the bellows. Never move the bellows without allowing air to flow freely, as this will adversely affect the airtightness of your instrument. Always be sure the air button, or a bass or treble button, is pressed when you are moving the bellows. Play a single note again and press the bellows, listen to the note. Keep the same button pressed and reverse the bellows, notice that the note has changed. Try another button and you'll find the same thing happens again. Each button plays two notes, one on the press and one on the draw. I hear you say "Time to pack it in, I'll never get the hang of this". Don't. Persevere, you will soon find yourself getting the correct bellows direction. I realise it seems an odd concept, but take my word for it, stick at it and you will soon be pleasantly surprised how the correct bellows direction comes so easily and naturally.

Time now to play something. I would like you to play a scale, doh ray me fah soh lah te doh. Select the third button away from your chin on the inside treble row with your first finger and press the bellows, now draw the bellows. Select button four with your second finger and press the bellows, now again draw the bellows. Repeat the press and draw selecting button five with your third finger. Next, select button six with your fourth finger, but this time keep the bellows on the draw, finally, press the bellows to complete the scale. Easy! You have just played the scale of G major. (The scale of some melodeons start on button four - I call these fourth button doh instruments - if yours is one of these, you will have to make the necessary adjustments of adding one to the button numbers.) Practise playing the scale a few times, both up and down, to make yourself fully familiar with it. Do the same on the outside row: this is the scale of D major. Now let's take a look at what you have achieved so far in musical notation.

The Scale of G Major

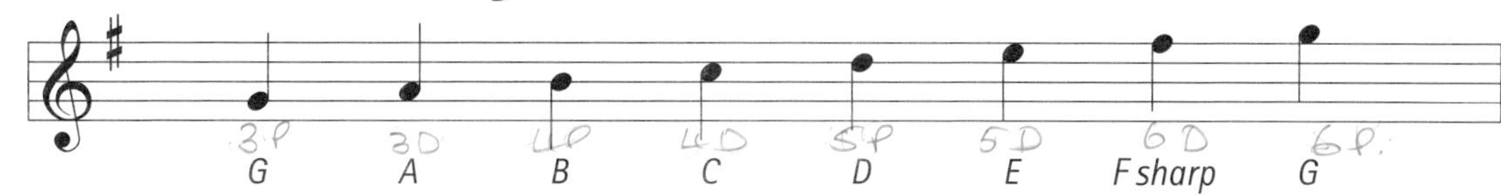

The Scale of D Major

Now try an easy tune, *Hot Cross Buns*. Play this simple tune on the G row, the inside row. To make it easy, the button number and the letter P or D, for press and draw, is written above each note. (Don't forget to adjust if you have a fourth button doh instrument.) Fingers one, two, three and four operate buttons two, three, four and five respectively.

Notice, that when playing this tune, it is difficult to keep the bellows open; you keep running out of air. A quick tweak of the air button when playing one or two draw notes in bar three will quickly redress the situation. This will be quite irritating at first but it's good to learn early. Using the air button in this manner is a way of life for melodeon players.

Hot Cross Buns!

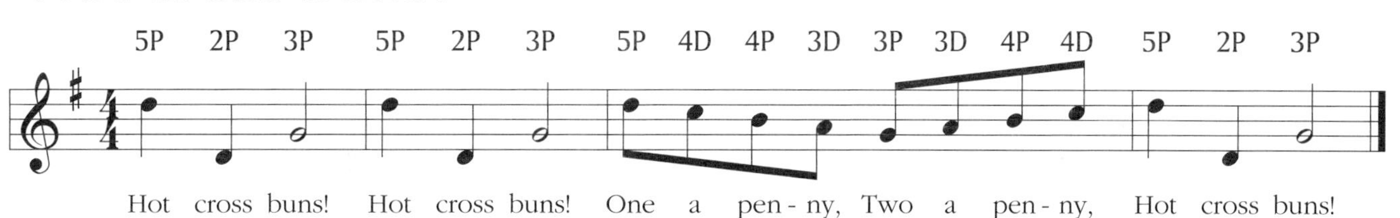

Holding the Melodeon

Some situations call for the melodeon to be played in the standing position whilst others allow you to sit down. Whether playing standing or sitting, it is vital to keep the keyboard firmly positioned. I always prefer to play seated. Sitting allows you to play with your thumb on the edge of the keyboard, giving maximum freedom to the playing fingers. When playing tunes requiring speed and dexterity this is a godsend. When playing seated it's best to use one fairly long strap. To keep the keyboard firmly in place, raise your right knee slightly higher than your left and rest the bottom of the grill against your right thigh. Alternatively keep your knees the same height and rest the grill against the outside of your left leg. When playing in the standing position, you will need to use two shorter straps, to keep the keyboard stable. Rest the keyboard in the crux of your first finger and thumb. Not having your thumb on the edge of the keyboard can be rather restricting but, with practice, you'll get by. Now, here's a problem situation that can easily arise and take you unawares. Don't expect to play standing up with any sort of expertise, immediately after playing sitting down for years. It will take considerable practice.

The Air Button

The air button is the most important button on the instrument. It is not there solely to facilitate opening and shutting the bellows without making a sound. It is there to keep the bellows within a carefully controlled range. For optimum playing performance, it is necessary to keep the treble and bass ends between fifteen and thirty centimetres apart. Any less than this and you're in danger of running out of air, any more and you'll lose control. It is vitally important during playing to be continuously caressing the air button, making constant adjustments, to keep the bellows within the limits of the ideal range. At first this can be quite difficult but, with experience, you will find that you do it as naturally as breathing. Often, it will be necessary to take an extra breath, so to speak, after or before a long series of notes occurring on one particular bellows direction.

The High Octave

The High Octave Scale of D Major

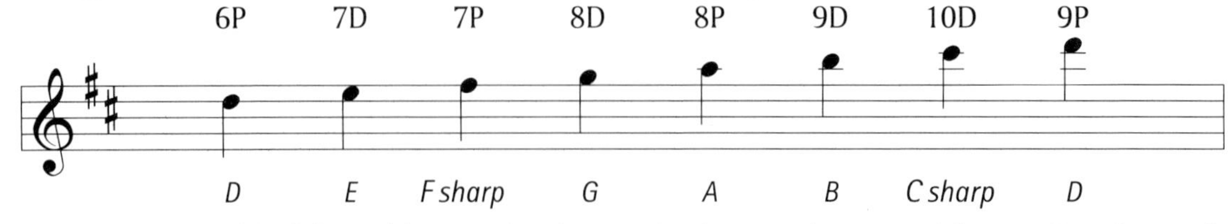

The high octave is rarely used in full on either row but is worth practising on the D row, to gain an understanding of it. Notice how the system is reversed to press/change/draw from the press/draw/change of the lower octave. Also, the last and highest note occurs back on the previously played button, where you might have expected to find a lower note. Five buttons are now required to accommodate this scale, rather than the four previously needed. Play button six press with your first finger, then button seven draw with your second. Next, replace your second finger with your first, to play button seven press. Button eight draw is played with your second finger, which remains to play eight press. Play nine draw with your third finger, ten draw with your fourth, then complete the scale by using your third finger again to play button nine press. It feels a bit awkward at first but you'll soon get used to it.

The Treble Buttons

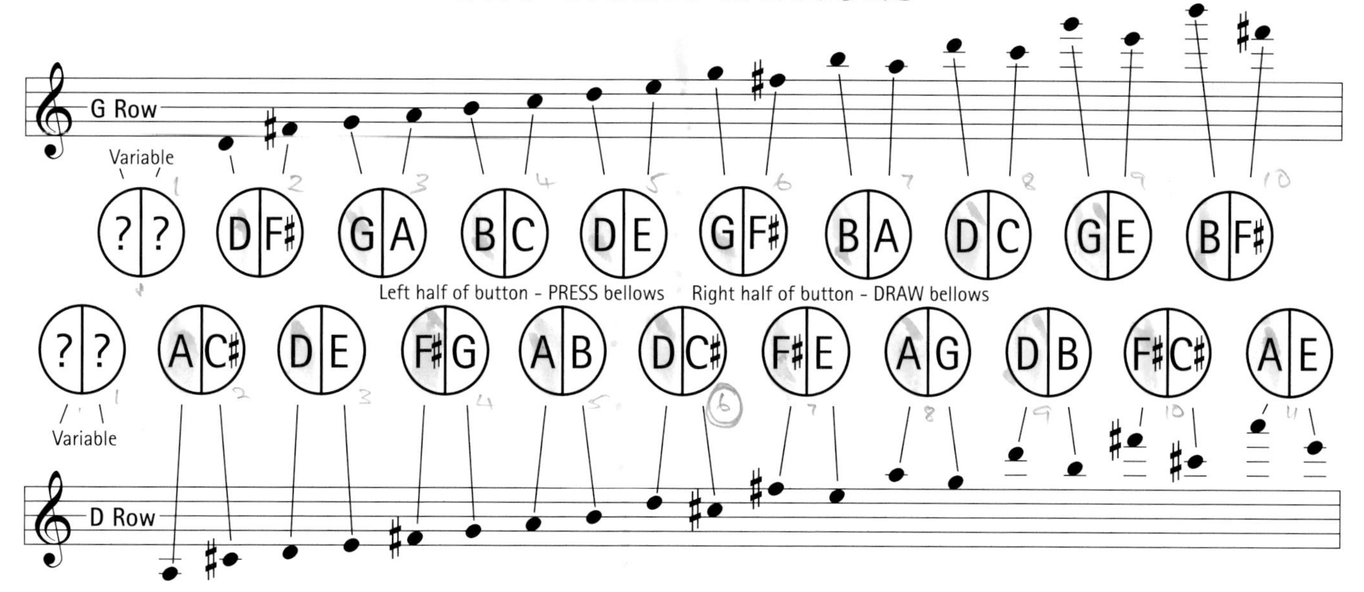

Examine the above diagram showing the notes produced by the treble, or right hand, buttons of the D/G melodeon. What does a theoretical evaluation reveal? It reveals a very unflattering picture of an elementary, incomplete instrument, that is incapable of producing all musical notes. An instrument consisting merely of two simple harmonicas placed side by side; only the scales of D and G are available. A severely limited instrument, that can only sound the notes of one scale plus one extra note. The chart tells a very sorry tale.

Pick up the instrument, play it for several years and become acquainted with its outstanding traits and characteristics. What does a hands on, practical approach reveal? It reveals a totally different story of a wonderfully versatile instrument, that has a range almost identical to that of traditional music, very much akin to that of the tin whistle, unkeyed wooden flute and uilleann pipes. Although it has a limited range, there are plenty of tunes that can be played on it, more than anyone could learn in several lifetimes. It is robust, loud if required, relatively light and compact, its press and draw system endows it with a natural rhythm, the basses make it self-accompanying, chords can be played on both treble and bass ends, it has a large volume range and, best of all, it is very easy for beginners to master.

Most of the music you will play, will be on buttons two to seven on the G row, and three to eight on the D row. Only twelve buttons of any consequence to deal with: certainly all the music in this book is played on these buttons. In fact, the vast majority of traditional music is played using only the fourteen notes shown below. Remember where to find these fourteen notes on the melodeon keyboard and, to all intents and purposes, you can read traditional music.

The notes played by the first button, or the first two buttons, of each row, can vary from one melodeon to another: they are often custom tuned to personal choice. It is not necessary for them to fall within the scope of this book. Suggestions as to what the notes might be are found on page 32. The last button of each row, shown on the diagram above, will be missing from twenty-one button, fourth button doh instruments. This is of no consequence as these notes are never required.

Time now to play another tune, *Baa Baa Black Sheep*. Bet you know this one. Play it on the D row, the outside row. When you see one sharp in the key signature, play on the G row: when you see two, play on the D row. Follow the cheating numbers and you can't go wrong. Use fingers one, two, three and four to play buttons three, four, five and six respectively. You'll notice some notes naturally last longer than others. The notes for "Black Sheep" last twice as long as notes for "have you any" and half as long as the note for "wool". Try and remember the time duration which each different note shape represents.

Baa Baa Black Sheep

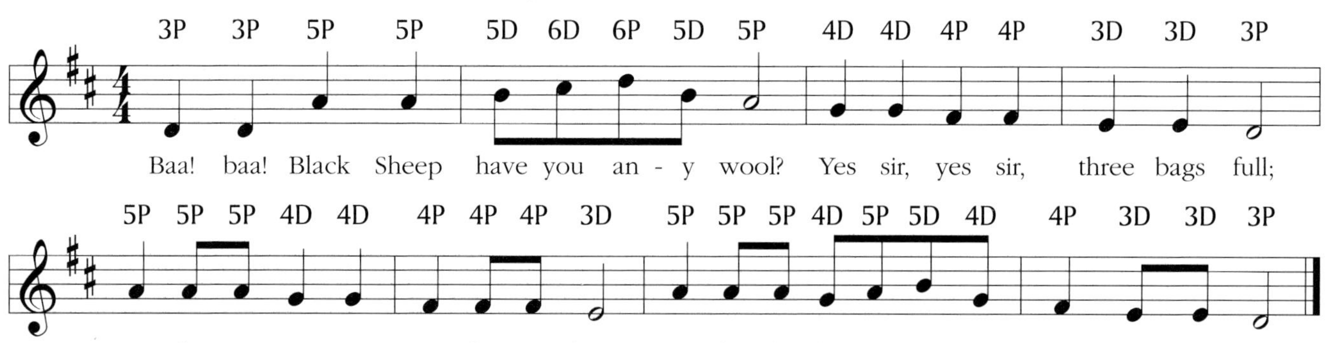

Counting Time

Here's a couple of short, easy tunes (complete with cheating numbers) for you to try. To facilitate ease and speed of learning, the tunes presented in the early stages of the book are all (if not, almost all) familiar melodies, words are included and you can hear the tunes on the soundtrack.

Let's try counting 4/4 time. Tap your foot at an even pace, say one tap a second, just as you would tap your foot whilst enjoying a piece of music. Count **1**, 2, 3, 4, **1**, 2, 3, 4 and so on, add a slight stress to **1**. Listen to the soundtrack: the tapping of the foot is represented by the clicking of the metronome. Each count is one crotchet, minims have two counts, semibreves four. Two quavers share a count; use the word "and" (say an') to count quavers that don't fall on the main beats.

Now play *Jingle Bells*. The sharp in the key signature, indicates that this tune is in the key of G, so play it on the inside row. It's dead easy, there are only three buttons to press. Use fingers one, two and three to press buttons three, four and five. Make sure you hold the semibreve notes on for a full count of four. Easy isn't it?

Now let's try counting 2/4 time. Count **1** an' 2 an' **1** an' 2 an', again with a slight emphasis on the **1**. Use the syllable "er" to count the semiquavers.

In traditional music, 4/4, 2/4 and 2/2 time signatures are very similar and are often interchangeable. In some music books the symbols **C** and **₵** are used to denote 4/4 and 2/2 time: treat them both as 4/4.

Now play *Little Brown Jug*. This time there are two sharps in the key signature, indicating the key of D. Play this tune on the outside row. Again, this tune is very easy, with only three buttons to press. Play it with fingers one, two and three, simple. Now play it using fingers two, three and four. You'll find this slightly more difficult. Devote plenty practice time to using these fingers, in order to develop and strengthen your little finger.

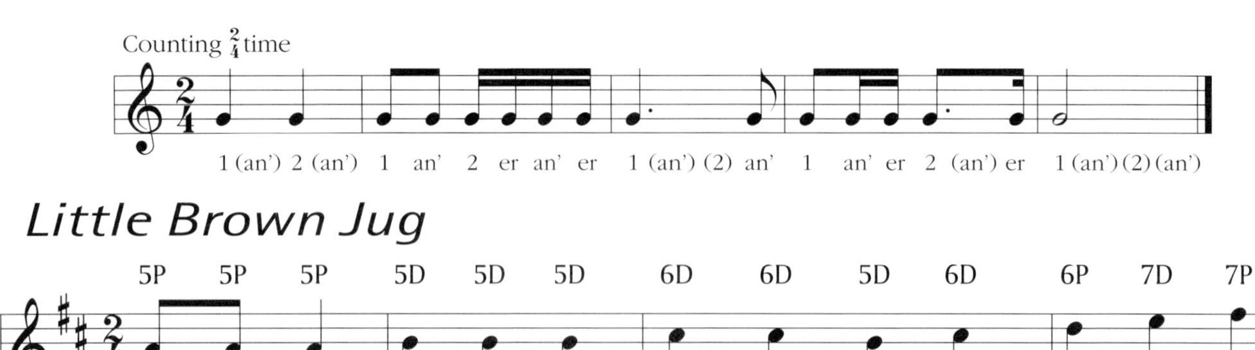

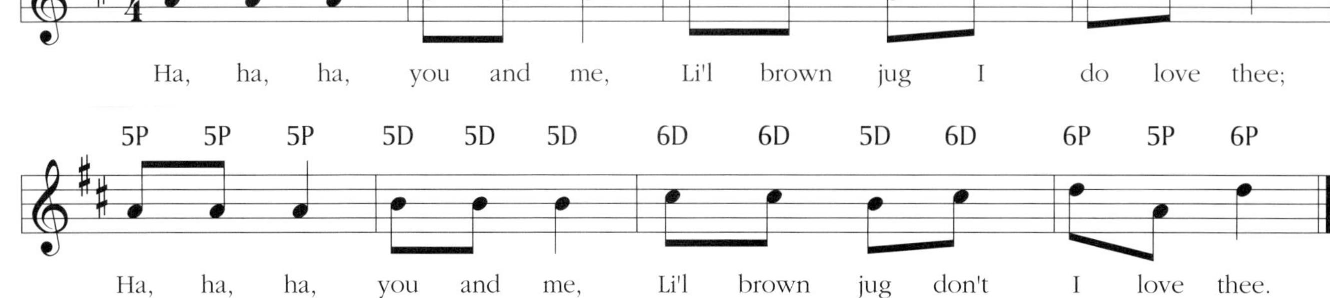

(an')

Counting Time

Here We Go Round the Mulberry Bush

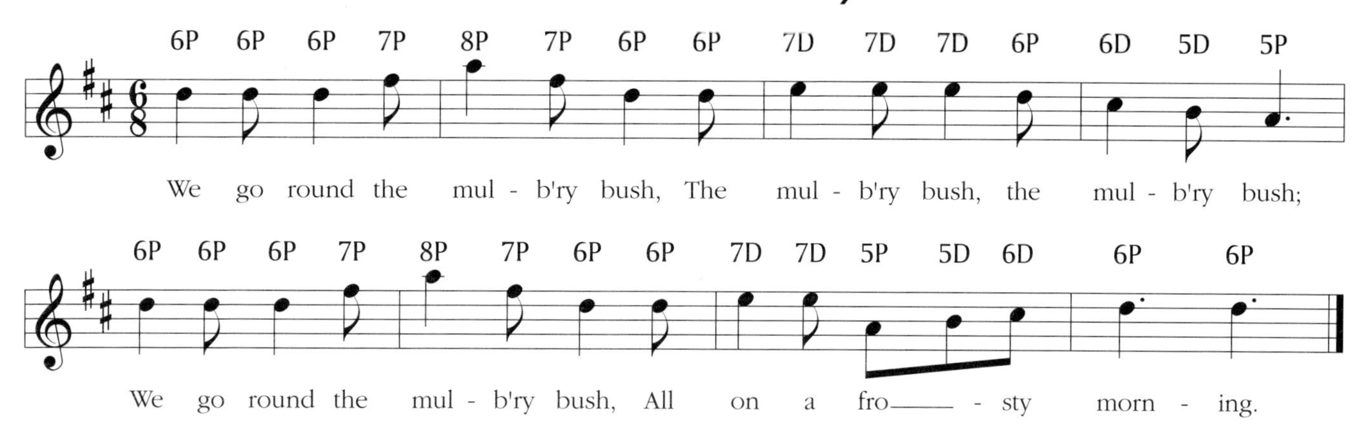

Now let's have a go at 6/8 time, six quavers to the bar, the time signature of jigs. It sounds a bit daunting but don't worry: it's quite simple and feels naturally suited to the melodeon. Although there are six quavers to the bar, there are still only two main beats, count **1** an' 2 an' **1** an' 2 an', in the rhythm of the words Humpty Dumpty, Humpty Dumpty.

Now play *Here We Go Round the Mulberry Bush*, it's slightly more difficult but it shouldn't cause too many problems. Listen to the soundtrack and make sure you've got the correct rhythm. There are two sharps in the key signature, so it's in the key of D; meaning, once again, we play it on the outside D row. You'll need to use fingers one, two, three and four to press buttons five, six, seven and eight respectively.

Practise *Mulberry Bush* until you can play it perfectly, without looking at the page. This is important. Written music is not used when performing traditional melodies; you will need to commit all your repertoire to memory. Written music is only used as a means of communicating tunes or, in the case of this book, as a medium to present information. Many top class traditional musicians can't even read music.

OK! Let's move on to 3/4 time, the rhythm of the waltz. Count 1, 2, 3, 1, 2, 3 etc.. Use an' to count the quavers.

Now play *Oranges and Lemons* on the inside row: it's in the key of G. It's so easy, fingers one, two and three play buttons three, four and five. You will need to make use of the air button on draw notes, to keep the bellows open.

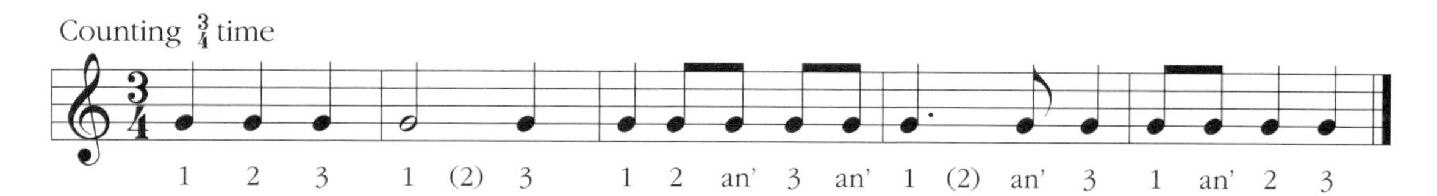

Oranges and Lemons

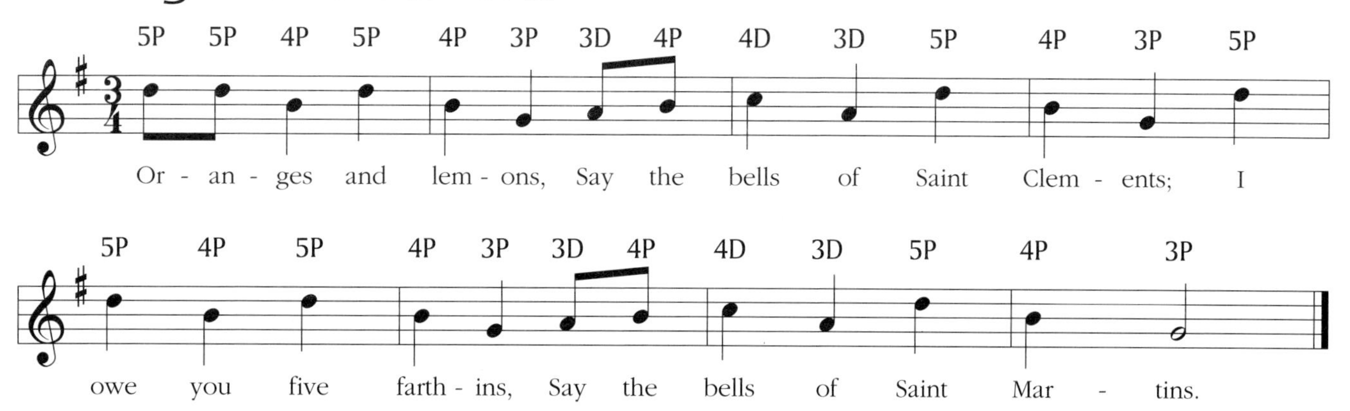

Major Keys

Bobby Shaftoe

On this page are couple of typical tunes, that can easily be played on the melodeon. Memorise and practise them, until you can play them easily from your head. Again, as usual, use of the air button is necessary, to keep the bellows in the ideal range. These tunes are in major keys, just the same as all the other tunes and scales so far. D major and G major are the main keys available on the melodeon: the key notes occur on the press of the bellows.

Bobby Shaftoe is an easy tune played on the inside row and should cause no problems. Don't forget to hold the minims on for twice the length of the crotchets. Notice that the cheating numbers have been omitted from the music. I'm sure you will be able to remember where many of the notes are by now, but if things get desperate, you can look them up on the chart on page 7. However, it's worth making a big effort not to look up notes you can't remember: try to work them out by playing the scale.

The first three notes surely cause no problem at all, they are the note G, the first note of the scale. Just have a think back to the *Music Basics*, page 4 and pull back into your memory, "*the names of the spaces spell FACE*", and "*after G start again at A*". If you know the names of the spaces, it's easy to figure out the lines, for instance B comes between A and C. Now play the scale and at the same time say G, A, B etc., until you have discovered where to play the next five notes. Coming up in bars three and four are a couple of notes we have yet to meet in the key of G; the note D, directly under the stave, and the note F, in the first space. You did spot the deliberate mistake, didn't you? Yes, correct. The ♯ symbol in the key signature tells us that all Fs are sharp, so the note is actually F sharp. But, where are these notes? They are obviously lower than the G note, so one would guess they are on the button nearer the chin and, sure enough, that's where they are; D is on the press and F sharp is on the draw. Just in case you didn't get all that, the cheating numbers are:

3P 3P 3P 4D | 4P 5P 4P 3P | 2P 2P 2P 3P | 2D 3D 2D 2P
3P 3P 3P 4D | 4P 5P 4P 3P | 3D 4D 3D 2D | 3P 3P

Use all four fingers to press buttons two, three, four and five.

On now to *Three Blind Mice*. You know the tune, so 6/8 time shouldn't cause any problems. Two sharps in the key signature means that F and C are sharp, no problem: play on the outside row where F and C are sharpened automatically. Again, don't look at the chart if you can help it.

First work out where to play the notes by playing the scale of D. Start on button three (outside row), play the scale and say D, E, F sharp, G, A, B, C sharp, D. You will soon have worked out that the cheating numbers are:

4P 3D | 3P | 4P 3D | 3P | 5P 4D 4D | 4P | 5P 4D 4D | 4P 5P
6P 6P 6D 5D 6D | 6P 5P 5P 5P | 6P 6P 6D 5D 6D | 6P 5P 5P 5P
6P 6P 6D 5D 6D | 6P 5P 5P 4D |4P 3D | 3P

Use your four fingers to press buttons three, four, five and six. Don't forget that the notes joined by ties are sounded as one, and to leave a slight gap where indicated by the rests.

Three Blind Mice

Minor Keys

Whip Jamboree

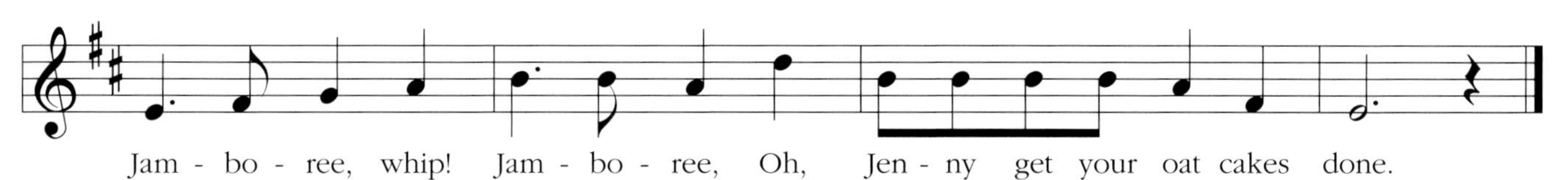

Here we have two more easy tunes, but this time in minor keys. With regard to the melodeon, minor key tunes can be roughly described as major key tunes turned inside out; they start and finish on the draw, whereas major key tunes start and finish on the press. The keys E minor and A minor are available on the melodeon, but E minor is generally regarded as the main one, because it has a bass chord specifically assigned to it.

To be strictly musically correct, the key signature of A minor has no sharps or flats, and that of E minor has one sharp. However, in the case of traditional music, A minor melodies almost always have F sharpened (meaning they fall into the scope of the melodeon), and E minor melodies usually have F and C sharpened. Therefore, although theoretically incorrect, in practice, you are likely to encounter A minor tunes written with one sharp in the key signature (play on the inside row), and E minor tunes written with two sharps in the key signature (play on the outside row). Some E minor tunes do have only one sharp; these are again played on the outside row, but it will be necessary to cross to the inside row to play the C naturals.

OK! We'll have a go at *Whip Jamboree*, a really great rousing sea shanty in the key of E minor. First of all work out where to play the notes on the outside row. Do this by running through the scale of D: you don't need to learn the scale of E minor. You'll soon work out that the cheating numbers are:

3D 4P 4D 5P | 5D 5D 5P 6P 6P | 5D 5D 5P 6P | 5D 5D 5D 5D 5P 4P
3D 4P 4D 5P | 5D 5D 5P 6P | 5D 5D 5D 5D 5P 4P | 3D

Use your four fingers to press buttons three, four, five and six.

On now to *Drunken Sailor*, probably the best known sea shanty of all. This tune is in A minor, so work out where to play each note on the inside row. If you are unsure, check your working against these cheating numbers:

5D 5D 5D 5D 5D 5D |5D 3D 4D 5D |5P 5P 5P 5P 5P 5P |5P 3P 4P 5P
5D 5D 5D 5D 5D 5D | 5D 6D 6P 7D | 6P 5D 5P 4P | 3D 3D

Oh dear! Did you run out of fingers at the end of bar six? You didn't really think that you could play every tune on four buttons? No, of course not. Almost every tune you play will involve shifting hand position. It's no problem; the secret is not to wait until the very last minute, you need to plan ahead. Just as when playing piano, good fingering technique is essential. The golden rule of good fingering is: **Always have a new finger available to play the next button, never play two consecutive buttons with the same finger**. There are several different methods we can use to manoeuvre our fingers round the keyboard.

So! How are we to shift hand position? Easy. Take a look at the note at the end of bar four and the note at the beginning of bar five, the ones with a 3 and a 2 above. They are the notes D and E, both are played on button 5, D is played on the press and E on the draw. When you've played D press with finger three, change to finger two to play E draw. This will ensure a finger is available to play the high A note coming later. It's as simple as that. To get your fingers back in position to play the low A at the end of the tune, a similar process in reverse is employed. Change fingers where indicated in bar seven.

Now is as good a time as any to start developing a good playing style. Tunes need to be played staccato, crisp and clear. There should be a slight gap between notes. It is important not to allow your music to sound mushy. Touch the buttons lightly and lift your finger off the button before playing the next. Keep this in mind whilst practising *Drunken Sailor*.

You have now encountered every note, except for two, that is required for all basic playing. It is important that these notes are committed to memory, in order to absorb the forthcoming information without hindrance.

Drunken Sailor

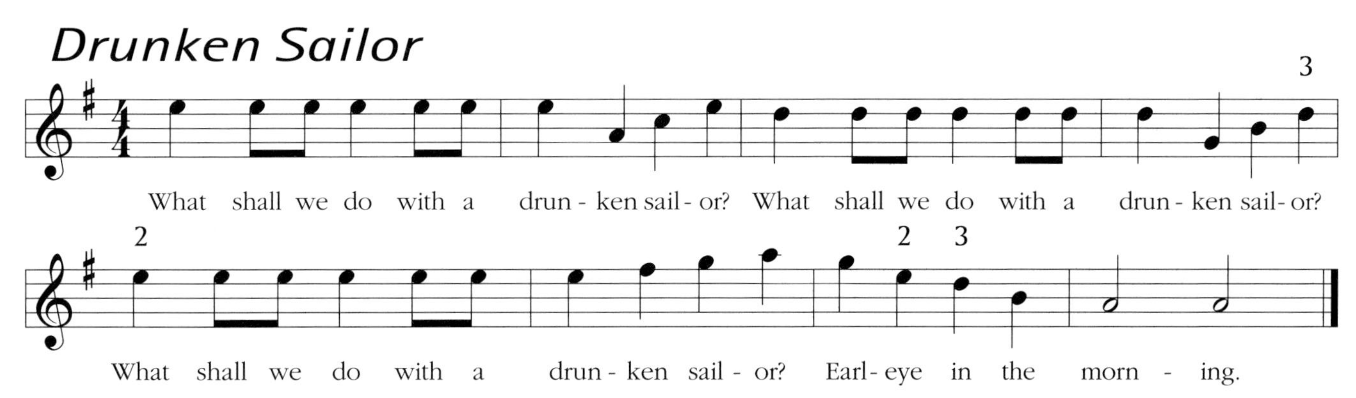

Shifting Hand Position

The numbers over the music no longer indicate which button to press but now represent which finger to use to play the note.

On this page we have two familiar waltzes, *Silent Night* in D and *The Best of Society Lives Down Our Way* in G. *The Best of Society* was originally called *Villikens and his Dinah*; many songs have been written to this tune, *Sweet Betsy from Pike* being one of the most notable. Both these tunes require shifts of hand position.

There are four basic ways of shifting hand position, **The Change** (┌──┐), **The Cross** (⌢), **The Stretch** (◄──►) and **The Miss** (⌒). Examples of each are found on this page and are indicated on the stave by the symbols.

We have already encountered **The Change** in *Drunken Sailor*. When a button is played twice in succession, a change of finger will move the hand by one finger. The manoeuvre can used to move the hand in either direction.

The Cross can be used in either direction. Going up: finger one crosses finger two to land on the button above; just as finger one is about to cross, finger two is withdrawn sharply. Going down, finger two crosses finger one to land on the button below; again, just as finger two is about to cross, finger one is withdrawn sharply. This manoeuvre will move the hand two fingers. It can also be executed using fingers two and three.

The Stretch is an obvious move and is simply a finger reaching further than the button it is hovering over. It can be used in either direction and can move the hand one, two or three fingers.

The Miss is when, rather than using the hovering finger to play a button, it is missed out and the next finger is chosen instead, moving the hand one finger.

The Best of Society Lives Down Our Way

Introducing the Bass Buttons

Don't think of your basses as consisting of eight buttons, but rather as four pairs of buttons in two squares. The square nearest the air button relates to the D row and the square furthest away relates to the G row. The main buttons are the two pairs nearest to hand, they can be named the main D row basses and the main G row basses. The button nearest the ground in each pair is called the **Fundamental** (Fun); it consists of two or three notes of the same name in different octaves, which is, effectively, a single note. The other button is called the **Chord** (Ch). It has the same name as the fundamental and consists of three notes, or four if the root note (the note the chord is named after) is added an octave higher. Almost without exception the fundamental is played on on-beats and the chord is played on off-beats. In all but 3/4 time fundamentals and chords alternate. Basic bass playing is to tap the basses exactly as portrayed below.

We now come across one of the melodeon's greatest assets. Once you have mastered the skill of tapping the basses in the above manner, whilst at the same time playing a melody with your right hand, you can be a one man band. Simply tapping out the rhythm on the main D or G row basses, according to the key, provides a perfectly acceptable harmonic accompaniment. Of course this can be improved upon, but the paramount concern is to get up and running as quickly as possible, before enthusiasm wanes.

OK! Let's practise some bass playing. Let's have a go at 2/4 and 4/4 time; with regard to the melodeon bass they are identical. The bass buttons are struck alternately in an even tempo; finger two strikes the fundamental and finger one strikes the chord in turn. Try it. Hear the basses sound like Um Cha, Um Cha, Um Cha, Um Cha etc.. Play your Um Chas to the rhythm of the words Glasgow Celtic, Glasgow Celtic. If you are unsure listen to the soundtrack. Practise this rhythm for several minutes on each pair of bass buttons.

On now to 6/8 time: it sounds quite complicated but it is much simpler than it sounds, and once the penny drops, it is easier to play than 4/4 time. Again, finger two strikes the fundamental, alternating with finger one striking the chord, but this time, in an uneven tempo. Between the fundamental and the chord is a slight gap, or there is a slight lingering on the fundamental. It's the Um Cha sound again, but this time, it goes to the rhythm of the word Dump - ty. Listen to the soundtrack and it will soon become clear. Practise this rhythm for several minutes on each button and hopefully, before long, you will agree with me that this is a very easy rhythm to play.

Finally, we'll have a go at waltz time, completing all the different rhythms required for traditional music. This time the basses are not played alternately, the fundamental is struck once with the second finger, then the chord is struck twice with the first finger. It goes to the One Two Three, One Two Three waltz rhythm that I'm sure you'll be familiar with. Practise this Um Cha Cha, Um Cha Cha rhythm for several minutes on each button.

You may prefer to use more fingers than just first and second to play the basses, some musicians use three and some four, but the majority, including myself, find that two does the job without hindrance.

Right! Let's try and fit some of what we have learned into a tune. Here we have *Frère Jacques*: familiarise yourself with the melody. Now play the melody and, at the same time, Um Cha the Glasgow Celtic bass rhythm on the main G row bass buttons. You should find the first line reasonably easy, just strike once on each crotchet and twice on the minims. Try singing to yourself Dor-mez Voo-**oo**, to remind yourself to strike the bass again before you leave vous. The quavers you will find a bit trickier; don't let the rhythm of your bass be dragged into the notes of the melody. You must stick doggedly to the bass rhythm, and only strike the basses on the first and third quaver of the bar. Listen to the soundtrack. I'm sure you'll soon get the hang of it.

Frère Jacques

Playing the Bass in Time

Egan's Polka

OK! You can just about get through *Frère Jacques,* keeping a steady bass going. That's fine. Let's quickly learn another tune while the going's good, to drive the lesson home. Notice that when you change the direction of the bellows to play the melody notes, the bass sounds change also, making a basic harmony possible without the necessity of changing buttons.

Egan's Polka is a great tune to learn. It's dead easy, and is a tune that you can use for Irish set dancing and English country dancing. You will hear it played in music sessions regularly. Notice that the tune consists of two parts and each part is played twice. This is typical of the tunes you will be encountering during your journey into traditional music.

First learn the melody. Notice how all the notes fall nicely under the fingers: shifting hand position is not necessary in this tune. Now bring in the main D row basses. Keep them nice and crisp and staccato, don't linger too long on the buttons, as this will reduce your music to a mush and take away the percussive aspect. The bass is there to provide both harmony and rhythm.

Each quaver takes one bass strike, the first and third of the bar taking the fundamental and the second and fourth the chord. Crotchets take two strikes. That's simple enough but, just so as not to make things too easy, some bars contain a dotted quaver followed by a semiquaver. Let's put these bars under the microscope and find out, in detail, exactly what is happening. I've split the crotchet into two quavers joined by a tie: it's exactly the same thing but it makes it easier to write in the bass. Likewise, the dotted quaver has been split into three semiquavers.

It's now easy to see just what is required to beat the bass correctly. We already knew to strike the bass twice whilst playing the crotchet, but what of the second half of the bar? We have two bass strikes left and two notes to play but, rather than the two notes taking a strike each, the dotted quaver takes two and the semiquaver takes nothing. Be careful to get this correct, and don't allow the rhythm of your bass to be dragged into the notes of the melody.

On to the waltz rhythm of *Oh Dear! What Can the Matter Be?* It's quite straightforward, no hand position shifting necessary. Play the main G row basses. The dotted minims take three bass strikes (Um Cha Cha) and crotchets take one. We'll take a look at bars two and three under the microscope.

I think this just confirms what you already know but, as you may have already noticed, I try to say everything at least twice. You may find waltz rhythm very easy to play on its own, but an impossible rhythm to keep going whilst playing the melody. Don't worry, this won't always be so if you keep practising. With practice you can, and will, overcome the impossible. I guarantee it.

Oh Dear! What Can the Matter Be?

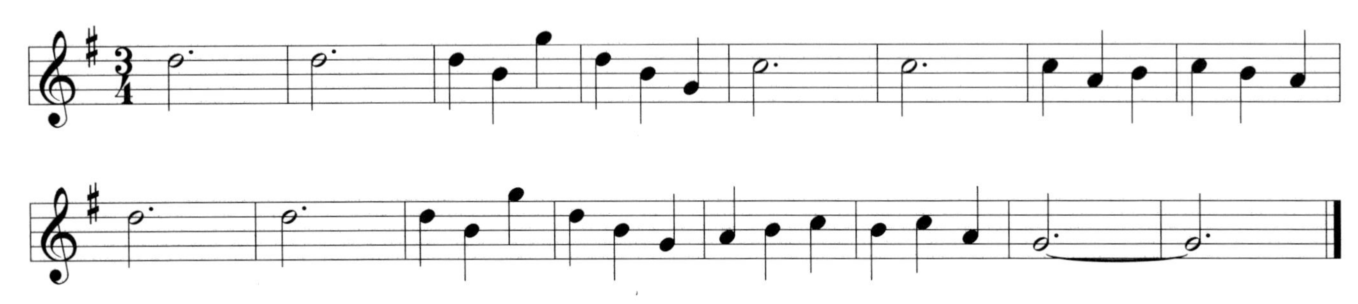

Playing the Bass in Time

Cock of the North

On now to 6/8 time. *Cock of the North*, the most famous jig ever. You know this one. Course you do: Aunty Mary, Had a Canary, Up the Leg of Her Drawers. See, I said you knew it. Another great tune for pub sessions, English and Scottish country dancing and, of course, *The Gay Gordons*. Again, we see there are two parts to this tune, and each one is played twice. The two parts are differentiated by various names: sometimes they are called first part and second part, sometimes first strain and second strain, sometimes A music and B music, and sometimes, the first part is known as The Tune and the second part is known as The Turn.

Learn the melody, consult the soundtrack if necessary, or why not try using *Humpty Dumpty* to get the rhythm. When you see the notes ♩ ♪ sing *Humpty*, when you see the notes ♩ ♪ ♩ ♪ sing *Humpty Dumpty*, when you see the notes ♫♪ sing *sat on a* and when you see the notes ♩.‿♩. sing a long *wall*, i.e. hold it for twice as long as in the nursery rhyme.

OK! Let's give it a try, just once through each part:

Humpty sat on a Humpty Dumpty, Humpty sat on a wa_all,
Humpty sat on a Humpty Dumpty, Humpty sat on a wa_all.
Humpty Dumpty, Humpty Dumpty, Humpty sat on a wa_all,
Humpty Dumpty, Humpty Dumpty, Humpty sat on a wa_all.

When you are fully conversant with the melody, have a go at fitting in the main G row basses. Just keep a steady Dump - ty Dump - ty rhythm going and you've cracked it. For crotchet quaver sequences, each note takes one bass strike. The tied dotted quavers take four bass strikes. Where there are three quavers together, only the first and third quaver takes a strike: the middle one gets nothing. Let's put the last two bars under the microscope, and find out in detail exactly what is happening. The dotted crotchets have been split into a crotchet and a quaver joined by a tie.

So there it is graphically. Make sure you miss striking the bass on middle quavers, and make sure you play four bass strikes on the tied dotted crotchets.

On now to *Katie Bairdie* in 4/4 time. *Katie Bairdie* is a hornpipe. The hornpipe is characterised by dotted quaver semiquaver pairs, and is played at a slower tempo than reels and polkas. The bass is played in the usual 4/4 manner, evenly paced alternate fundamental and chord beats, but the main beats are played in a more emphasised and pronounced manner. Here are the words: the syllables in bold indicate where the main beats (fundamental strikes) fall:

***Ka** - tie Bair - die **had** a coo, **Black** and white a - **boot** the moo,*
***Was** - n't that a **dain** - ty coo? **Dance** Ka - tie **Bair** - die.*

Let's examine the first bar under the microscope and see where the bass strikes fall. Use the main D row basses.

Fun Nothing Ch Nothing Fun Nothing Ch

You can see that playing the bass is quite a tricky business but, don't forget, you can achieve the impossible with practice. Notice no bass is played on the semiquavers. When playing hornpipes you must be ultra careful not to strike your basses in the dotted crotchet semiquaver rhythm, this will effectively turn the hornpipe into a jig. Listen carefully to the soundtrack to become accustomed to the rhythm, then practise until perfect.

Katie Bairdie

Various Rhythms

The Keel Row

Hornpipe Time

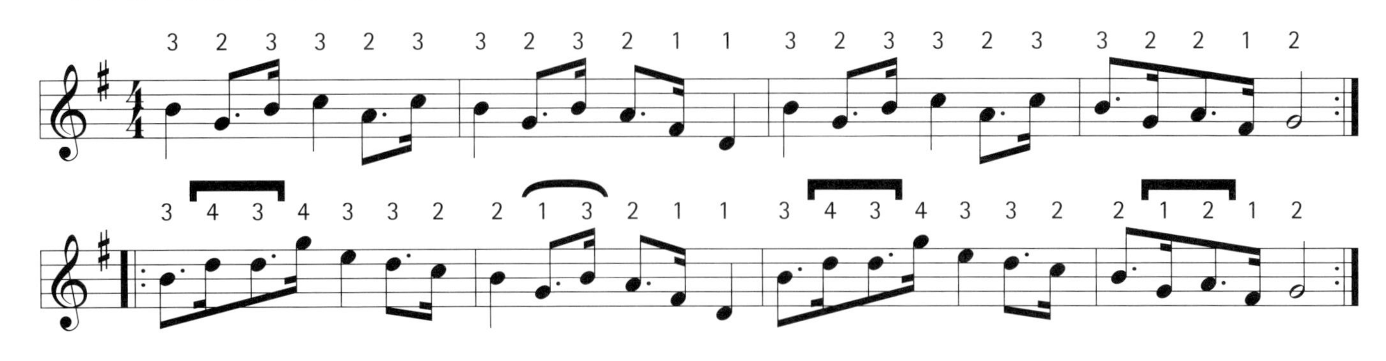

The Keel Row

Reel Time

Unlike classical music, traditional tunes are not written on tablets of stone; they can be interpreted in a variety of ways. As was mentioned earlier, 2/4 time and 4/4 time are often interchangeable. Many reels when slowed down turn naturally into hornpipes, jigs when slowed down can easily be turned into waltzes, and so on. Traditional tunes can have major changes made to them, like we see on this page with *The Keel Row* being played as a hornpipe, reel and march. Other changes can be more subtle, for instance notes can be added, deleted, lengthened or shortened for variation, to help with fingering or for simplification to make playable.

Play these different variations of *The Keel Row* using the main G row basses. Listening to the soundtrack will demonstrate how to interpret these different rhythms. Where indicated, use **The Change** and **The Miss** to shift hand position in the second part.

Play the bass in a similar manner to *Frère Jacques* and *Katie Bairdie*, making sure to give two bass strikes to minims and four strikes to semibreves. We have under the microscope bar seven of Hornpipe Time, bar eight of Reel Time and the last two bars of March Time.

When you are familiar with the tune, have a go at playing bars three and four of the hornpipe in the following manner and, perhaps, try some of your own variations.

The Keel Row

March Time

Crossing the Rows

Polly Put the Kettle On

Polly Put the Kettle On is in the key of G: we play it on the inside row. Notice that bar four contains the note E, on the bottom line of the stave. This note is not available on the G row. In order to play the note E, when playing on the inside row, you must cross the rows and play it on the outside D row, button three draw. You have no choice. It's possible that you have an instrument which has an E on the G row as well as the D row. Even with such an instrument, it is still usually better to play the E note on D row. It is certainly better to choose the D row for the E note, anywhere it occurs in this book.

As you progress, row crossing will become more and more common. So, from now on, to accommodate this, the finger number over the music has now been joined by the letter D or G, to indicate on which row the note is to be played. For anyone not paying complete attention, I'll **shout** it:

The numbers and letters over the music will not help you find where to play the notes. They are there to indicate on which row to play the note and which finger to play it with.

You should find *Polly Put the Kettle On* a quite straightforward tune, even with the row crossing. When you are familiar with it, bring in the main G row basses. Play them in a similar manner to *Frère Jacques* and *Katie Bairdie*. Let's put the last two bars under the microscope.

Skip to My Lou is the easiest tune ever, so it should cause no problems at all. However, it is a useful tune to introduce a couple of fundamental techniques that can be put to constant use. Use the main G row basses.

Play the tune through, carefully following the fingering indicated and ask yourself, why have two hand position shifts been employed, when it wasn't necessary to make any? This is because, whenever possible, it's best to have your four fingers hovering over the lower scale of either row, then you know exactly where you are. I call this position the **Home Position**, always try to get back to the **Home Position** as quickly as possible. Of course, as you can imagine, this is open to much interpretation, personal preference and exceptions that prove the rule.

Below, bars seven and eight are under the microscope. Note the the quaver that doesn't take a bass strike, and don't forget to give two bass strikes to the minims.

Bar seven has a rather awkward series of notes, some tricky quick quavers. To play them all on the same row, a bellows reversal is required for each. However, simply by playing the B notes on the D row (button five draw) instead of the G row, the whole series of notes will now occur completely on the draw. Bar seven is now much simpler and smoother. You will encounter this manoeuvre constantly.

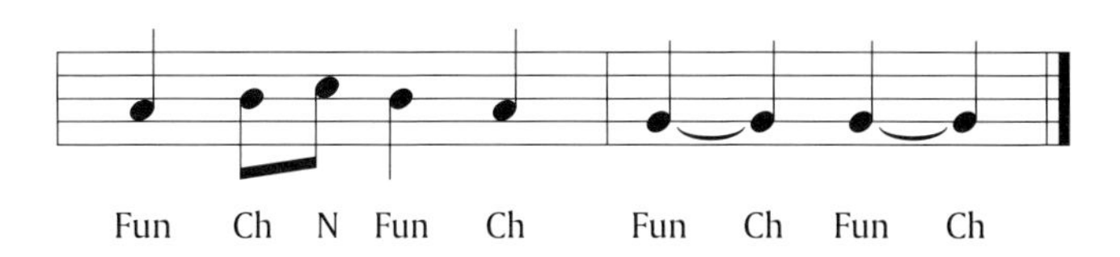

Skip to My Lou

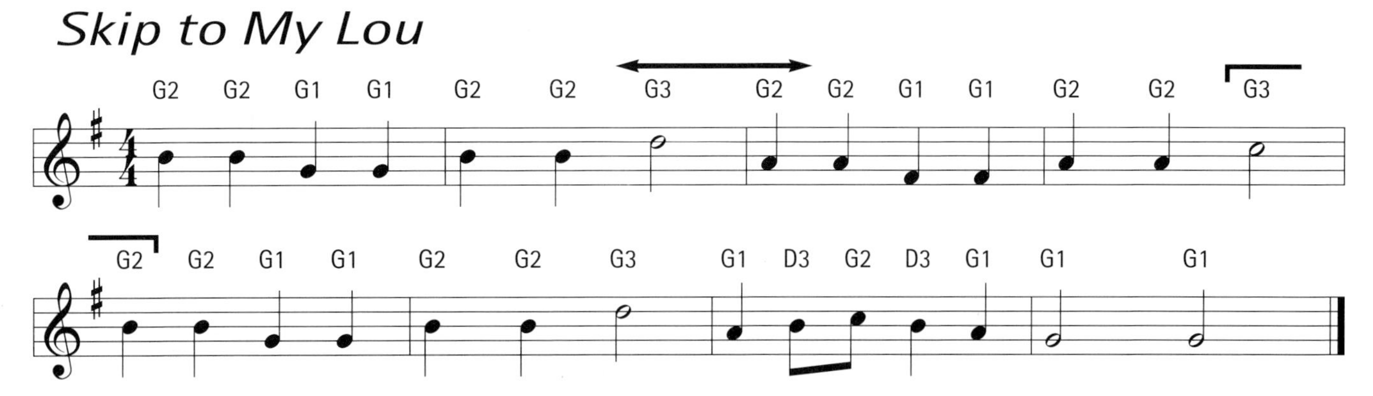

The Basses

Now you are able to play the bass in time, it's time to try and improve the harmonies. First of all we need to know what the basses are. We already know that each pair of basses consists of a note and a chord. We now need to know their names. Below is a chart showing the names of the bass buttons. The view is the same as seeing the bass buttons from the playing position. The left half of the button represents PRESS bellows and the right is DRAW.

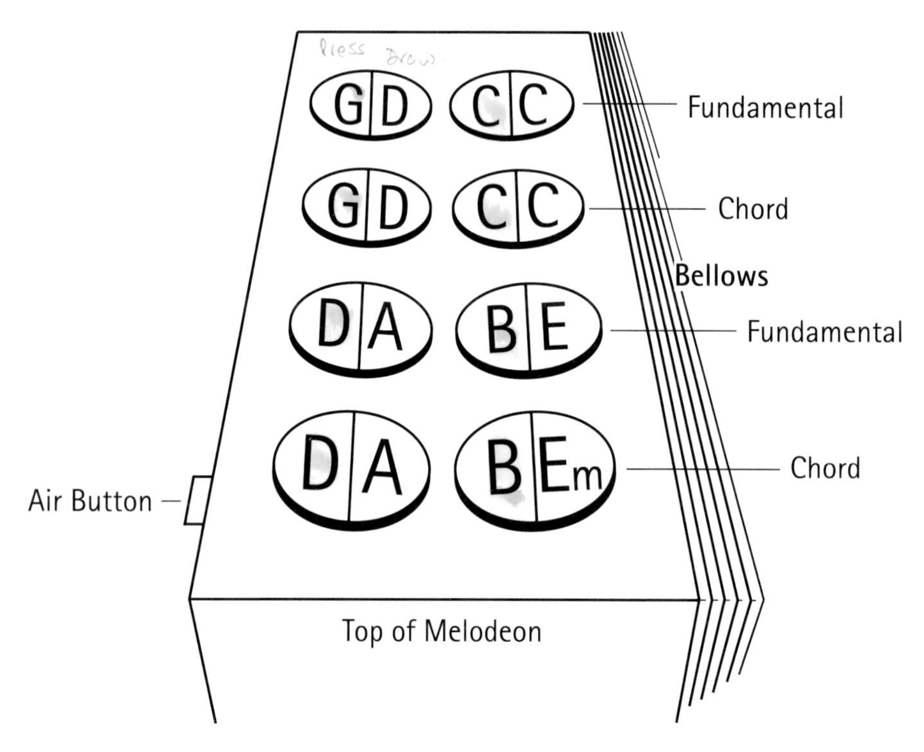

What notes do the chords consist of? Major chords consist of the root note, plus the third and fifth notes of the major scale named by the root note. It's the same for minor chords, except that the third is flattened by one semitone.

It's easy to work out the notes in a chord using your right hand palm up. Count your fourth finger as one and onwards to your thumb at number five. Say the major scale as you tap each digit. The notes of any major chord will occur on your fourth finger, second finger and thumb; the first, third and fifth digits in the series. Try it with the major chords.

First	Second	**Third**	Fourth	**Fifth**
Fourth	Third	**Second**	First	**Thumb**
G	A	**B**	C	**D**
C	D	**E**	F	**G**
D	E	**F♯**	G	**A**
A	B	**C♯**	D	**E**
B	C♯	**D♯**	E	**F♯**

Lastly we'll do it with E minor: it's the same process, only remember to flatten the third.

First	Second	**Third**	Fourth	**Fifth**
Fourth	Third	**Second**	First	**Thumb**
E	F♯	**G♯→G**	A	**B**

The notes in the chord of G are G, B and D
The notes in the chord of C are C, E and G
The notes in the chord of D are D, F♯ and A
The notes in the chord of A are A, C♯ and E
The notes in the chord of B are B, D♯ and F♯
The notes in the chord of Em are E, G and B

Before moving on, let's try a few bass button exercises, as shown below, to strengthen the fingers. The bass buttons are represented musically, as well as by the more usual chord symbols. It's best to play the D basses on the press and the C basses on the draw. This will even out the press and draw sequences. However, just for the practice, you can also play them in the opposite directions. There's nothing complicated about these exercises: just tap out one Um Cha on each chord in the sequences indicated. Play each sequence for several minutes before going on to the next. Then repeat the exercises in 6/8 and 3/4 rhythms. You can hear the exercises on the soundtrack.

Playing the Other Bass Buttons

Shepherds' Hey

Now, yet another dimension is added to the music. Chord symbols have been appended below the stave. Such chord symbols will be found on most music you will encounter. These chord symbols indicate which basses to play.

Note, in the music above, the short bar at the beginning of each line: this is quite usual. Most tunes start just before the main beat occurs, so there is usually a short lead-in bar at the beginning. The sum of the notes in bars of music is always equal to the amount indicated by the key signature, thus bars of 4/4 time contain four crotchets-worth of notes. The value of notes in the lead-in bar will be found to be missing from the last bar, to even things out. The lead-in bar becomes part of the last bar on repeating.

On now to *Shepherds' Hey*, a nice, simple Cotswold morris tune. Study the fingering and learn the melody thoroughly. Notice the use of **The Change** at the end of each line, to get straight back to the **Home Position**. Also, notice the quick deviation to the D row in bars three and seven, to avoid the quick bellows reversals. In particular, notice how the first three notes of each line are played, G1 D3 G2, it's the same manoeuvre we used in bar seven of *Skip to My Lou*, except this time, the bellows direction is press rather than draw. This manoeuvre occurs time and time again in both directions and I have named it the **Half-Diamond**. This is because a line drawn round the three buttons played, will take the shape of half a diamond.

Now let's take a look at the bass. Bar one: the crotchets get one G bass strike each; then reach to the C basses to give two strikes on the minim. Bar two: strike the G basses on the crotchets; when the bellows are reversed the D basses will automatically sound. Bar three: play the basses like bar one; the last note doesn't receive a bass strike. Bar four: select the D press basses this time; play the G fundamental on the last note, then sound the chord on the first note of the lead-in bar. The second part is identical.

OK! Let's play *Tralee Gaol* and make use of the E minor basses. The tune is played all on the D row. Only two easy hand position shifts are required, **The Stretch**, to reach the first note of the second part, and **The Change**, going from bar fourteen to bar fifteen.

Let's bring in the bass and take a look at what's happening. Probably a good lesson to learn at this point is that it is impossible to be spot on with the chords all the time, but when they err, they still sound fine. Note all the times we are caught on the wrong direction to play the Em. Also note how the dotted notes keep the bellows in the correct direction, just long enough to play the correct harmony. Let's put bars fourteen and fifteen under the microscope.

D Fun N D Ch N D Fun D Ch E Fun N Em Ch N D Fun D Ch

Tralee Gaol

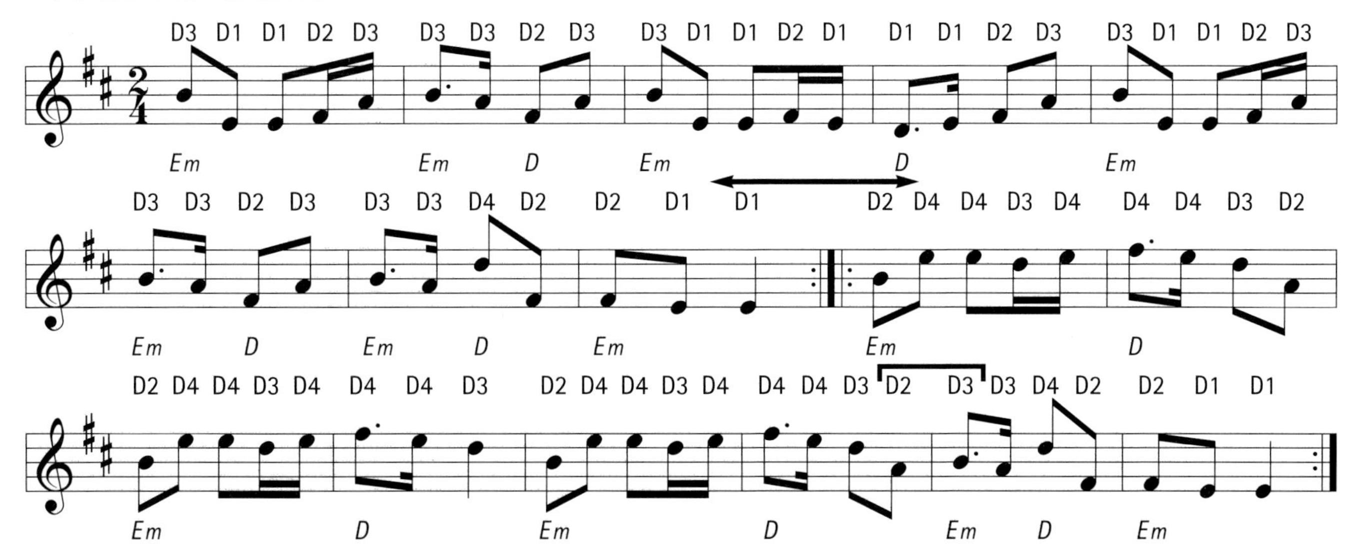

Um Cha Through Some Easy Tunes

I Have a Bonnet Trimmed with Blue

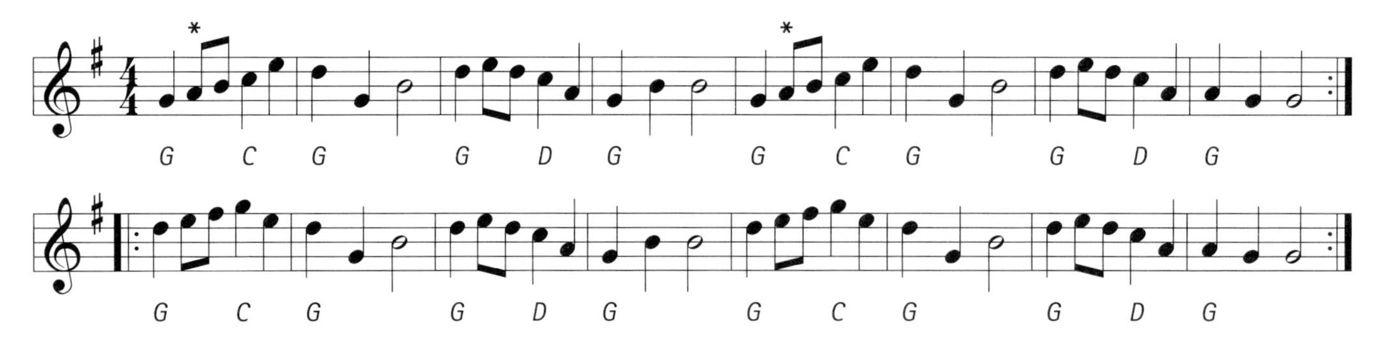

Donkey Riding

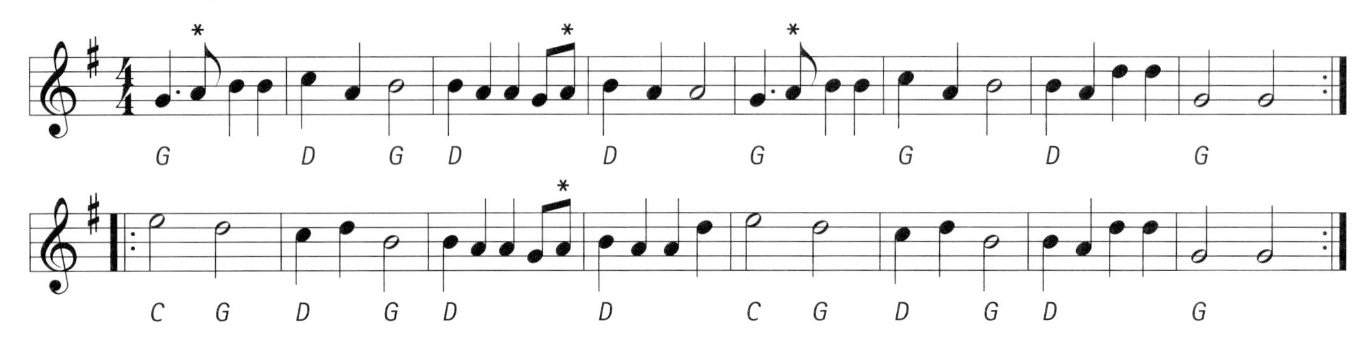

Time now to take a break from the grind and bash out some easy tunes, using some of the techniques learned so far. Four tunes to go at, all in the key of G. They are all valuable tunes to have in your repertoire, because they crop up regularly in pub sessions and are all useful country dance tunes.

Play these tunes using the **Half-Diamond**, by playing the A and B notes, marked by asterisks, on the D row with finger three. Tap away in the usual Um Cha manner on your basses. Play the main G row basses throughout, ignore the occasions when the bellows direction is incorrect, but be sure to change to the C basses where indicated by the chord symbols. Note that when we play the C basses, the bellows direction, for the most part, tends to be draw. Relax and have fun playing these tunes. Notice in *Buffalo Girls*: you will have to use **The Change** to shift hand position in bar fourteen, so you have enough fingers to play bar fifteen. In bar sixteen, use **The Change** to bring your hand back to the **Home Position**.

Buffalo Girls

Uncle Bernard's Polka

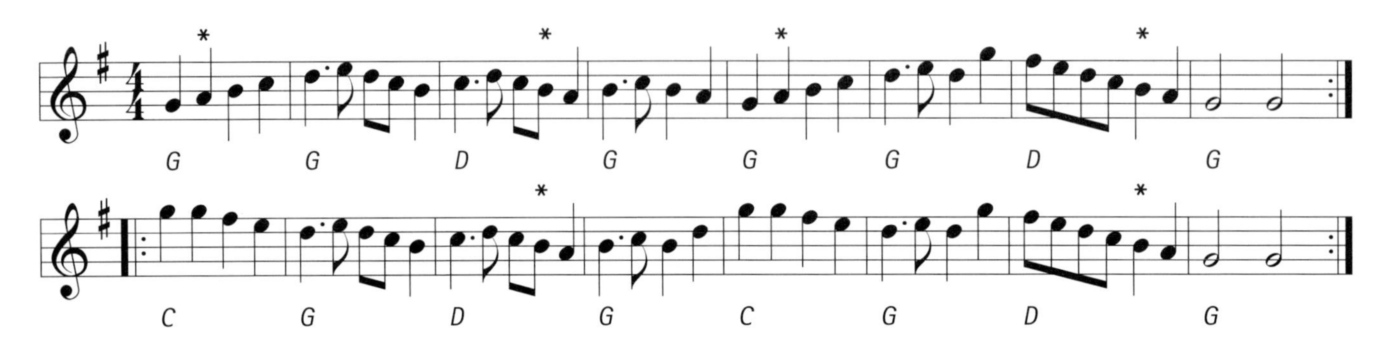

Smoothing the Bellows Action

Rakes of Mallow

Some melodeon players favour using the instrument's press and draw characteristics, to produce a punchy, rugged style of playing. Others prefer to use row crossing techniques, to smooth out the action of the bellows. I would suggest that the best style of playing is a mixture of both. Some tunes, or sections of tunes, sound best using press and draw techniques, while others sound more pleasing when smoothed out. Some passages of music can be almost impossible to play using one technique, whilst becoming relatively simple using the other. What style you adopt is your decision, but bear this in mind; habits are difficult to break. You'll find, after learning a tune thoroughly, it is much harder to re-learn it using a different fingering than it was to learn it in the first place. Try to play tunes "correctly" right from the start.

On now to two really well-known tunes, *Rakes of Mallow* and *Davy Davy Knick Knack*. Just about every traditional musician knows them, so they are well worth learning. Playing these tunes totally on the G row requires a substantial amount of bellows work. Playing the tunes with a smooth bellows action requires some difficult finger work. Try playing these tunes using both methods; you have the knowledge to easily work out the "one row" style, and the fingering is written in for the "smooth" style. Also, try playing the tunes using a mixture of the two methods. Work at the tunes until you are happy with your fingering, then practise them to perfection. I'm sure that you will need these tunes time and time again over the years.

Both these tunes sound fine using only the main G row basses for accompaniment, played in the usual Um Cha manner. However, notice in bars nine, ten and eleven of *Rakes of Mallow*, every time we hit the chord button, the bellows are travelling in the wrong direction to play the correct chord of G. You can be really clever here and just keep tapping the fundamental button, to replace the chord with the note D. The note D is one of the notes that form the chord of G, thus a genuine harmony is created. Use a similar technique in bars thirteen and fourteen, return to normal bass playing in the second half of bar fourteen, Um Cha the basses whilst playing the D crotchet.

Davy Davy Knick Knack

The Other Chord in the Key of D

Twinkle Twinkle Little Star

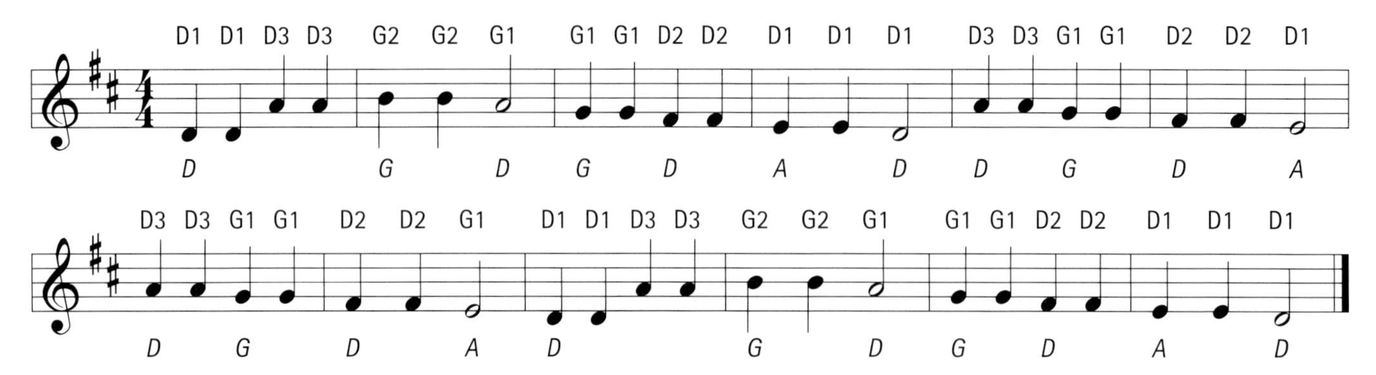

If you are dabbling in a few other tunes, as well as the ones in this book, it wouldn't be surprising if you are often left feeling frustrated, because you are unable to play the third chord in the key of D. In key of G tunes, we simply had to reach across to play the C basses. When playing in the key of D we find the equivalent basses have been replaced by Em. Let's explore.

Every key has three main chords, often known as the three chord trick, **Tonic**, **Sub Dominant** and **Dominant**. These chords are always named by the first, fourth and fifth notes of the scale; they can be easily worked out using the fingers of our right hand, in the same way we worked out the notes of the chords on page 18. This time the answers are on finger four, finger one and thumb. Let's first confirm that this works, by finding the chords in the key of G. Fourth finger G, third A, second B, first C, thumb D. Sure enough the notes on finger one, finger four and thumb are G, C and D. It works: we already know that the chords in the key of G are G, C and D. If you try it for the key of D, you will note that the chords are D, G and A. So, we now know that G is the elusive chord. Perhaps things aren't quite as bad as we first thought, because we have a G chord: unfortunately it's on the wrong bellows direction. Let's explore further.

If you take a look at tunes with chords appended, in this, or for that matter, any other traditional music book, you will notice that, on the whole, the notes any particular chord is played against, are mostly the same notes as those of which the chord is comprised. The chord of G, as we already know, is made up of the notes G, B and D. A quick glance at the keyboard diagram (page 6), tells us that all these notes can be played on the press of the bellows. So, rather than attempting the impossibility, of playing the G chord on the draw, let's play the G, B and D notes on the press instead.

OK! That's enough chat. It's time to play some music. To introduce the chord of G into the key of D, we'll go back to the simple stuff, and what could be more simple than *Twinkle Twinkle Little Star*. Follow the fingering over the music and see that we play the B notes in bar two, on the press of the G row, rather than the draw of the D row. This makes the G basses available. I'm sure that's exactly what you were expecting, but it's the next note, the A, that is the most interesting. Rather than going back to the D row, play it on the G row draw instead. You can play the D basses on either bellows direction. If you use the press notes in order to accommodate the G basses, it is often necessary to find some D chord notes (F♯ and A) on the draw, to redress the balance of press and draw notes. If you don't, you will soon find yourself in the embarrassing situation of having no air left in the bellows. The rest of the tune is now obvious.

Compare the chords of G and Em (page 8). You will notice that they are almost identical, G, B, D and E, G, B. It won't now come as a surprise to find out that G and Em are often interchangeable. Play this beautiful Cotswold morris tune from Bampton, *Bonny Green Garters*, using both Em and G basses to accompany the same phrase. Learn the tune using the fingering indicated. Notice we play bar two (don't count the lead-in bar) B A B on the draw and bar six B A B on the press, allowing us to play Em basses the first time and G the second. Notice how we use row crossing to shift hand position in bar three. Another good way to play bar three, is to use **The Change** on the first note, and use the fingering D2 D2 D2 D3 D3 D4. Notice that the middle note in the groups of three quavers is often on the wrong direction to play the correct bass, but the outcome remains unaffected because no bass is sounded on these notes. Note **The Cross** in bar five.

Bonny Green Garters

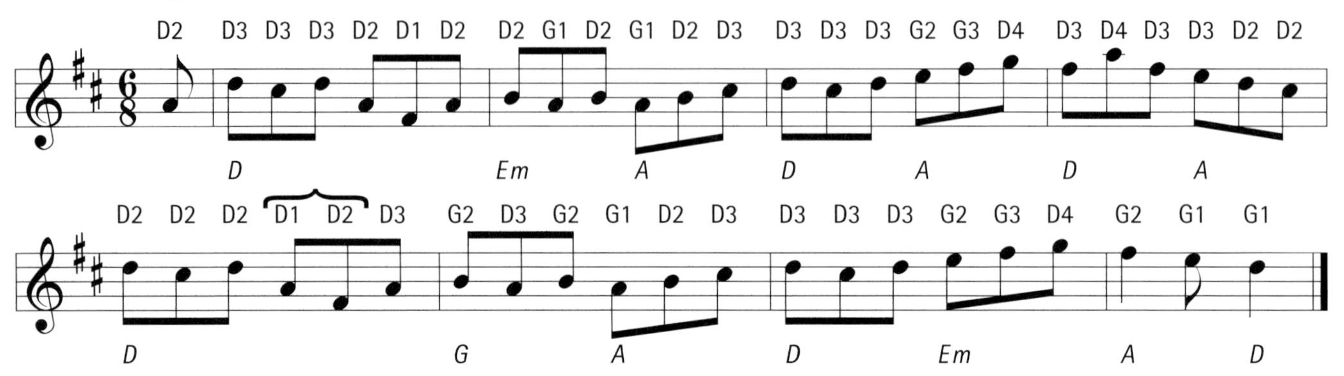

Fundamentals and Chords

Rodney

Well! You've certainly come a long way since starting out on this book. If you've religiously followed the book, step by step, and you are proficient on all the tunes presented, you will, by now, be a reasonably accomplished player. If you've done it in under two years, congratulations, that's good going. Most students will have taken much longer.

Right! Time to move on now. Here's another Cotswold morris tune I'd like you to learn, *Rodney*. This tune is from the village of Headington. Learn the tune thoroughly using the suggested fingering. Note the use of the **Half-Diamond** three times in the first bar and a half. Now let's fit the bass. Play the main G row basses throughout the first part and second half of the second part, no problem. Bars five to eight are slightly trickier because, where D basses are indicated, rather than relying on the bellows reversals, to let the D basses kick in automatically, I want you to change to the D press basses. Now let's put that under the microscope and see what we've played.

Notice that every time we want to play the D fundamental, we are caught on the wrong bellows direction, forcing us into playing an A instead of a D. This is no detriment because the note A forms part of the chord of D. We've just substituted the fifth as the fundamental instead of the root and, in doing so, kept the harmony accurate and avoided the alternative incorrect harmony of D Fun G Ch.

In the second half of the first bar we find the chord of D. Let's investigate the reason why this chord has been selected. The previous page told us, chords are played against passages that contain a predominance of notes that constitute the chord. However, for the dominant chord, we use the notes that constitute the seventh rather than the straight forward major chord. To melodeon players, this simply means, include a C with the notes of D major, the dominant chord in the key of G. Include a G with the notes of A major, dominant chord in the key of D. Include a D with the notes of E major, dominant chord in the key of A. Thus the D chord has been selected because the notes C and A occur in the chord of D7.

OK! Moving swiftly on. *Liza Jane* is a great tune for American square dances. There's a lot happening in this tune, so make sure to give it your full attention. First, listen to the soundtrack to get the melody firmly in your head, because bars three, seven, eleven and fifteen are rather tricky. Notice the use of the A fundamental with the D chord in bars one, three, five and eleven. In bars four and twelve, note that you are required to play the A note on the G row draw, so that the A basses sound, rather than the D basses. Notice that in bars seven and fifteen we cross to the G row for the F♯, then slide across the rows to play the E note. This puts the bellows on the draw. Play the D draw basses Um Cha then, half way through playing the F♯ note, change to the A basses and play Um Cha. In bars ten and fourteen, play the B note on the G row, in order to play the G press basses. Don't forget the long D notes in bars nine and thirteen take three bass strikes, and the long D note in bar sixteen takes four bass strikes.

Liza Jane

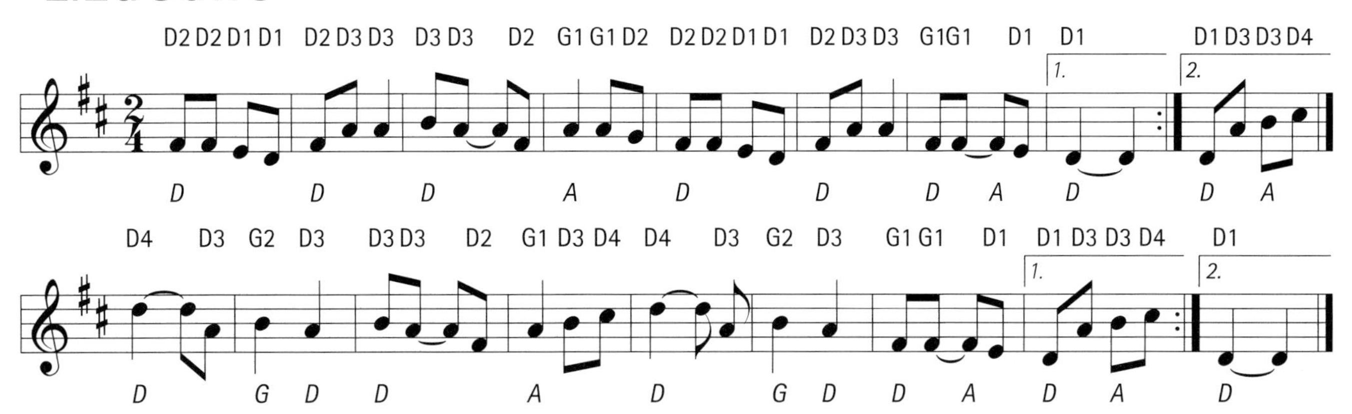

Playing the Bass in Harmony

Constant Billy

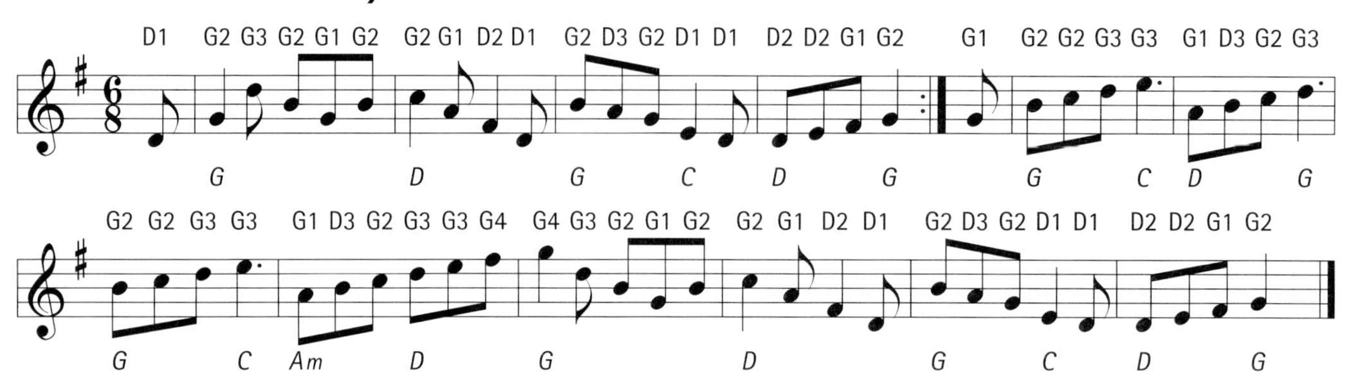

Right! Let's play these two smashing Cotswold morris tunes, *Constant Billy* from Adderbury and *The Twenty-Ninth of May* from Headington. We'll look at some other techniques to keep the bass in harmony.

But first, note the new manoeuvre for shifting hand position in bars three and eleven (don't count the lead-in bars) of *Constant Billy*. Instead of using fingers 2, 3, 1 to come down the **Half-Diamond** we use fingers 2, 3, 2, shifting the hand one finger. Going up the **Half-Diamond** use fingers 1, 2, 1 instead of 1, 3, 2 to move the hand one finger up. Other **Half-Diamond** movements are: fingers 2, 3, 2 going up and 1, 2, 1 coming down: both bring the hand to the **Home Position**.

Look how nicely our fingers fall on the buttons in bar two of *Constant Billy*: C and A notes, G row draw, then F♯ and D notes, D row press. Um Cha the D draw basses, then Um Cha the D press basses. Fitting the D basses into bars four and twelve requires a little more dexterity. Play the D press fundamental with finger two; then shift basses and play the D draw chord with finger two; next play the G press fundamental, again with finger two; finish by playing the G press chord, against the D note in the lead-in bar, with finger one. Notice that the first strike of the C basses is on the press and the second is on the draw. No problem. Our C basses are the same on both directions.

Use the same technique to play the D basses in bar eight as you used in bars four and twelve. That's OK, but what's this Am? Unfortunately the D/G melodeon bass doesn't have room for an A minor chord. However, it does have the A fundamental. The trick here is to drone the A fundamental and not to strike the major chord. It makes quite a good effect. Why not try it with other basses?

OK! On to *The Twenty Ninth of May*. It has a rhythm similar to that of *Katie Bairdie*. The first part doesn't hold any surprises, but it's worth mentioning, that in bar two, the C chord suggested could be replaced by Am or D. Also, the fingering could be changed to G2 G1 D3 G2 G2. In other words, there's more than one way to harmonise or finger a tune and still be equally correct; a point well worth bearing in mind. Play the last note of the first part with finger one, when going to the second part, but use finger two, when returning to the beginning.

On now to the second part. Here we see something new, lower case letters under the music. These letters represent single notes, i.e. the fundamentals. So, in bar seven, we have a bass run rather than chords. The treble notes E, D, C, B are played simultaneously with the fundamentals C, B, A, G. In the next bar, return to normal bass playing, making sure that you Um Cha on the D draw basses, then Um Cha on the D press basses. Note the slide from F♯ to E.

The Twenty-Ninth of May

Playing the Bass in Harmony

Sweet Jenny Jones

On this page we have a Welsh waltz and an Irish double jig. Double jigs are characterised by a predominance of groups of three quavers, whereas single jigs have a predominance of crotchet quaver pairs.

Let's first take a look at the waltz, *Sweet Jenny Jones*. Notice the use of dotting notes, as in *Tralee Gaol*, to hold the bellows direction until the chord is struck. Notice that where A basses are required, we always play A notes on the G row draw. Note that the Em chords in bar fifteen are preceded by the B fundamental, the fifth instead of the root.

Now for *My Darling Asleep*, a difficult tune for experienced musicians, so don't expect to master this one in a couple of days. Here's a useful tip: **Learn your tunes slow and accurate; only when you can play them spot on slowly is it time to gradually bring them up to normal tempo.**

Notice how the carefully worked out fingering takes us easily round the keyboard: all the time keeping the bellows in the right direction to play the correct basses, and we always have a finger available to play the next button. Notice how we start on the D row press, then a bellows reversal automatically sounds the C♯. See how we then use the A note on the G row to keep the bellows in the draw direction. This allows use of the A basses, and also manoeuvres our fingers into position to play the B and G notes on the G row press, in order to sound the G basses. Reversing the bellows is all that is required to play the next note and, moving back to the D row, puts us briefly in the **Home Position**. We then use **The Cross** to take our fingers back up the keyboard to play the high notes in bar four, all on the draw, allowing us to play the chord run Em, A. We then use **The Cross**, to come back to the **Home Position** and start the second part. Now note the crafty bit of fingering used in bars nine and ten. It's usually wise to avoid playing several repetitions of the same note with the same finger. Although we're not about to run out of fingers, we use **The Change** to relieve finger three, then **The Stretch** to get back to the **Home Position**. What about the wrong bass in the lead-in bar? We'll let that pass. When it comes to melodeon basses, there's no way you can win 'em all.

My Darling Asleep

Percussive Bass : No Bass

The Steamboat

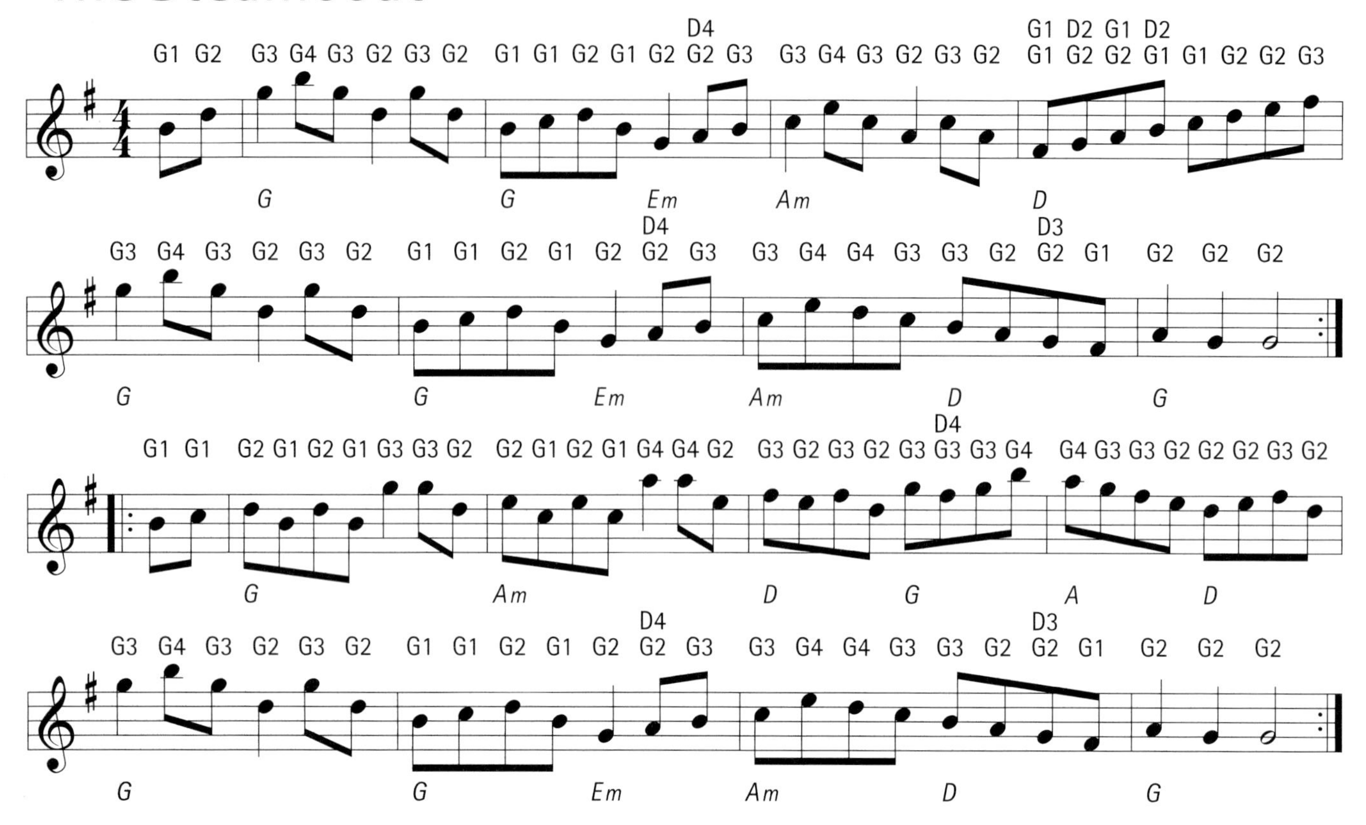

For most tunes, achieving a perfect harmonic bass can be impossible or too burdensome. Repertoire is king in traditional music: there's simply not enough time to learn every tune with a fantastic bass harmony. One way to get round this problem is to just tap the basses lightly and create more of a percussive effect than a harmony. Try this technique in *The Steamboat*. This tune is more often played slower with a dotted rhythm as a hornpipe, but here I play it at a faster pace, more like a reel. Play it all on the G row or, if you prefer, use the alternative fingering where indicated, to smooth out the bellows action.

Anyway! Why play bass at all? You don't play bass if your instrument is fiddle, banjo or flute. Besides your bass may ruin some accompaniment backing from a guitarist or pianist. In other words, you are not compelled to keep an incessant Um Cha Um Cha pounding on, throughout each and every tune, on every occasion. It can become extremely irritating sometimes, to listeners and other musicians. Try backing off your bass somewhat and, to start with, let's go all the way and learn *Sonny's Mazurka* without tapping the bass at all. This is a lovely tune, so why spoil it. A mazurka is of Polish origin adopted by the Irish: it can be thought of as a waltz with lots of notes.

You might wonder why I have suggested using **The Change** in bar one, only to return to the **Home Position** in bar three; there was no shortage of fingers. It is essential to use **The Change** in bar five. So, using **The Change** in bar one, keeps our fingering alike for the two identical phrases, avoiding confusion. Crossing to the G row in bar seven is not essential, but seems easier than staying on the D row.

Sonny's Mazurka

Drones and Snappy Off-Beats

Speed the Plough

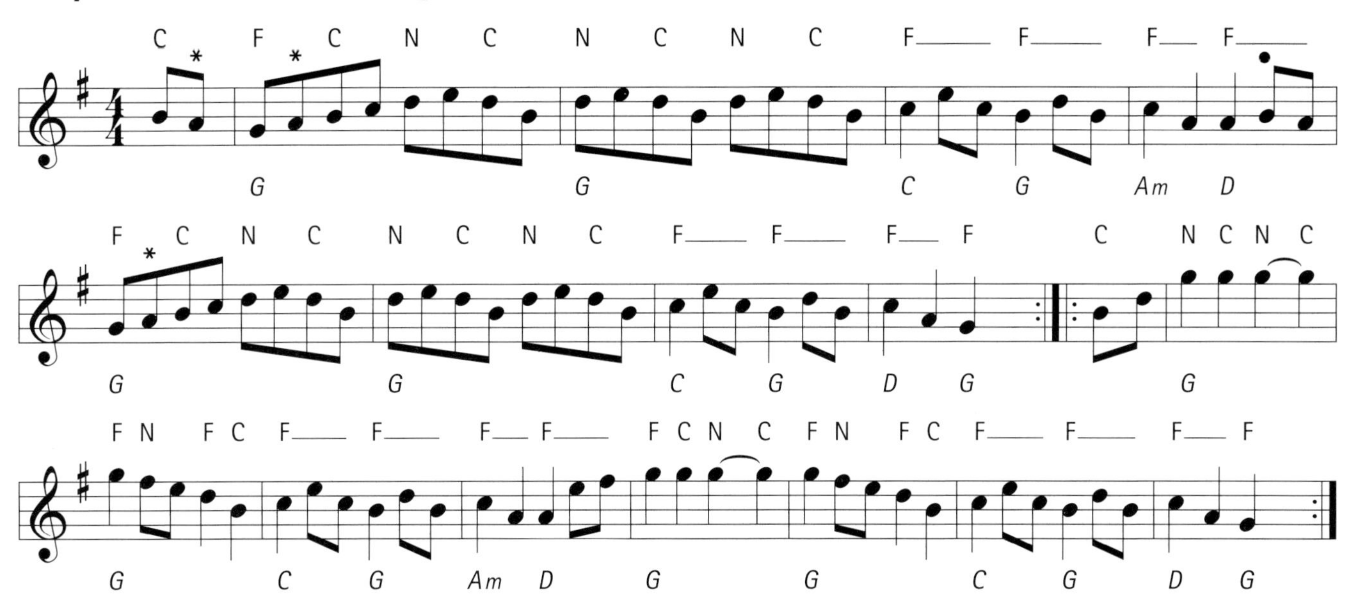

Soldiers' Joy and *Speed the Plough* are probably the two most popular and best known tunes heard at English pub sessions. Learn these tunes using some rather more tasteful bass techniques. Instead of playing Um Cha Um Cha all the time, miss out some bass strikes. Let some of the fundamentals sound a little longer than normal and leave out the chord in some passages. In other passages, avoid the fundamental totally, just play some quick, snappy taps of the chord on the off-beat.

In practice, you'll just make it up as you go along, but on this occasion, have a go at reproducing these tunes exactly as I have played them. F means tap the fundamental of the suggested chord, F____ means drone the fundamental and C means tap the chord. N indicates a point where normally the bass is sounded, but in this instance, is left silent.

Speed the Plough is a fairly easy tune and is played all on the G row, except the A notes marked by an asterisk and the B note marked by a dot. Play the A notes on the D row using the **Half-Diamond**, and also play the indicated B note on the D row with finger three. You'll probably find it quite painstaking work to transfer the information on the page to your head, but persevere. I'm sure you'll find it worthwhile.

Soldiers' Joy is a bit more complicated than *Speed the Plough*, so the fingering has had to be written out in full. Make sure you have the melody well and truly in your head before attempting to bring in the bass.

Don't let the Am and Bm chords bewilder you. Notice that, where these chords are indicated, you are only required to drone the A and B fundamentals.

Soldiers' Joy

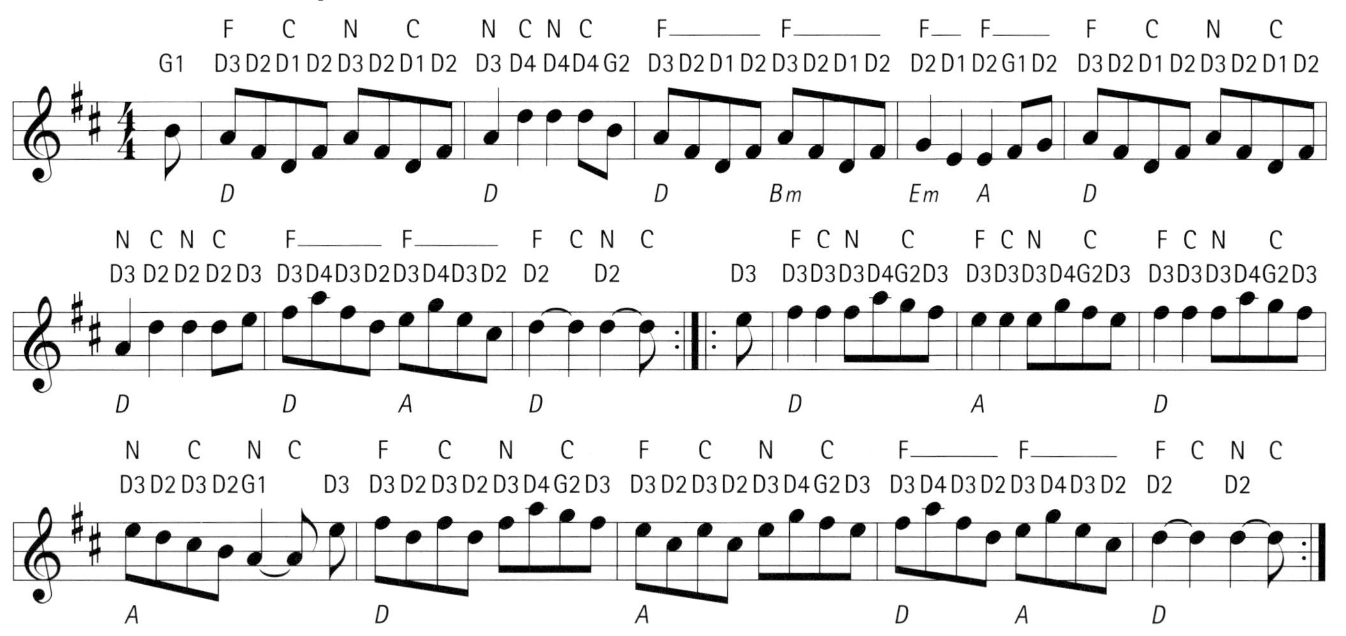

Accidentals

Staten Island

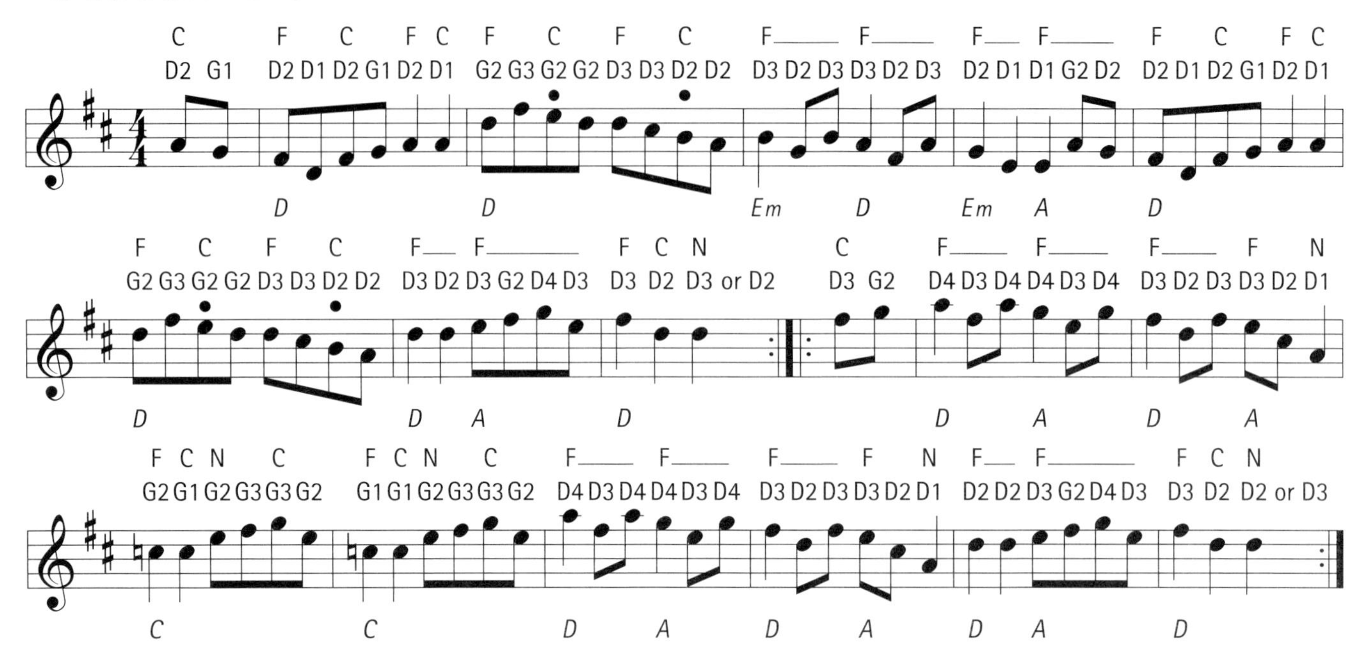

Sometimes, tunes contain notes that are foreign to the scale indicated by the key signature. These notes are known as **accidentals** and are indicated by sharp, flat and natural signs, which apply to all following notes of the same pitch up, to the end of the bar. As often as not, these accidentals can be found on the other row, and here we have a couple of good examples.

First we have *Staten Island*, a reel in D, with a C natural accidental. Use the full Um Cha bass technique in bars one, two, five and six. This disguises the incorrect harmonies we are forced to play, by the notes (marked by dots) that stubbornly occur on the opposite bellows direction to that of the correct chord. Notice that striking this wrong chord has no detrimental effect: the music still sounds great. Notice the frequent occurrence of the **fundamental, chord, nothing, chord** sequence in both *Soldiers' Joy* and *Staten Island*, a very useful standard bass pattern to keep in mind.

A Trip to the Cottage is an Irish double jig in G, with a C♯ accidental. Notice in bar eight we alternate fingers one and two to play the three G notes, a very useful technique. Make a mental note and use it when necessary in other jigs. Use the normal Um Cha Um Cha bass but drone the C and D fundamentals in the penultimate bar. Rather than playing the A fundamental, where an A minor chord is indicated, play your C basses in the normal Um Cha manner.

The notes in the chord of C are C, E and G. The notes in the chord of Am are A, C and E. They are very similar chords, they are often interchangeable and they don't sound discordant when they are played together. The chords Em and G bear the same relationship. The notes in the chord of G are G, B and D. The notes in the chord of Em are E, G and B. The same applies to the chords of D and Bm. The notes in the chord of D are D, F♯ and A. The notes in the chord of Bm are B, D and F♯.

A Trip to the Cottage

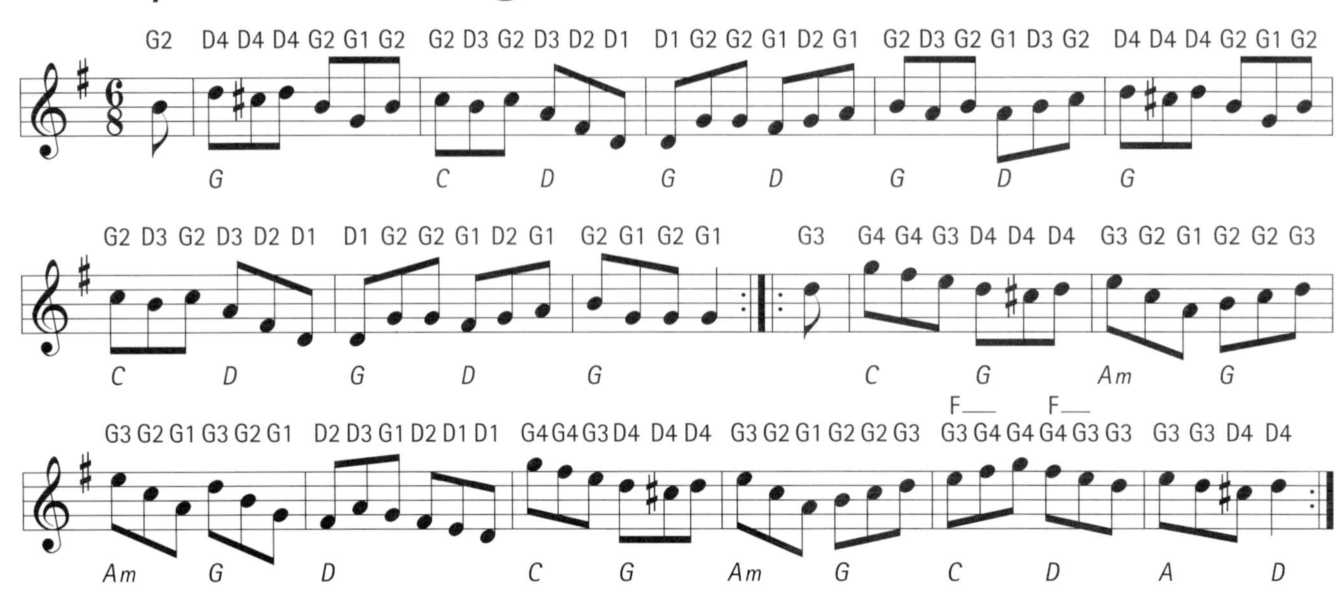

The Keys of A minor and B minor

The Tenpenny Bit

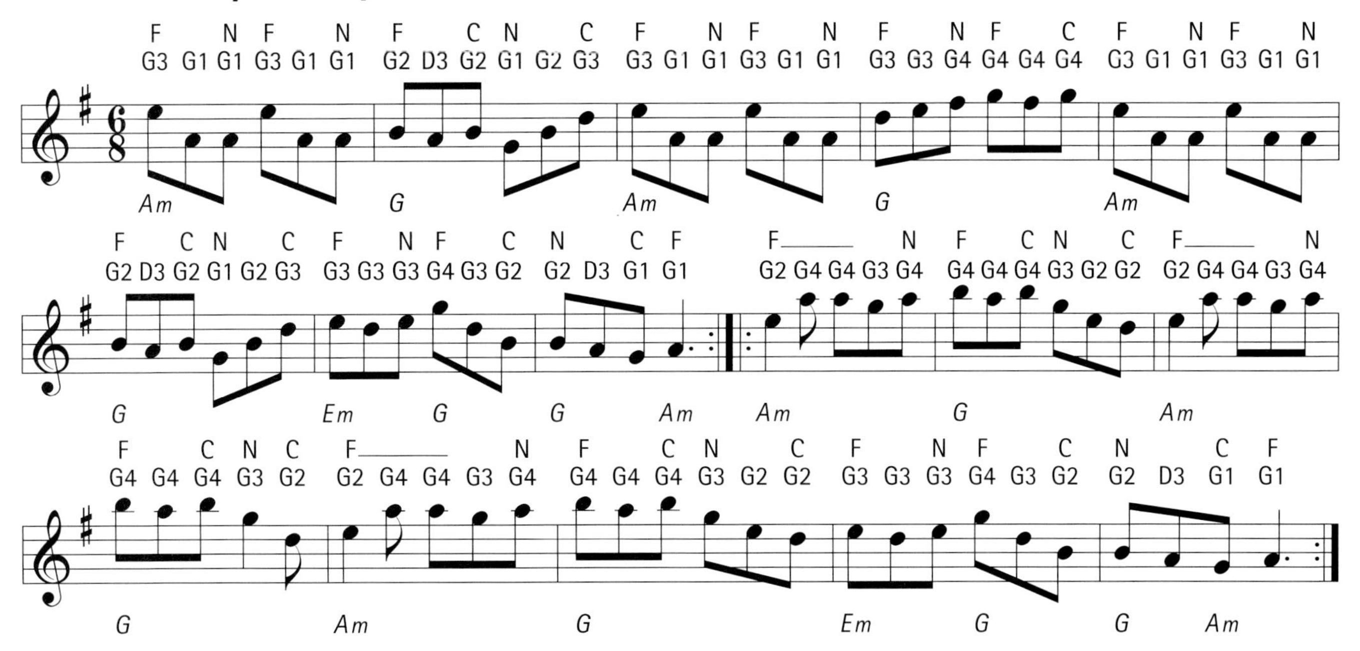

You will encounter the key of A minor frequently in traditional music. The key of B minor also crops up quite regularly but rarely remains in place for the whole of a tune.

Here we have another Irish double jig, *The Tenpenny Bit*. It's in the key of A minor: play it on the G row. Unfortunately, the C chord is not a suitable substitution for Am, when the key is A minor. Therefore only the A fundamental is available for use, when we are required to play an Am bass. This means we have to work out a bass line that is sympathetic to the fundamental only Am basses. My solution is written over the music above. Notice the **fundamental, chord, nothing, chord** sequence cropping up again. Also note the use of the A fundamental drones in the second part, to simulate the Am chord.

Right! Let's move on to *Tripping Upstairs*, yet another Irish double jig. It's a brilliant tune that turns up regularly in both English and Irish sessions. The first part of this tune is totally in the key of D. In the second part the key changes to B minor, but by the end of the tune, the key has reverted back to D. As would be expected, the key of B minor presents us with exactly the same problems we had with the key of A minor. We can only use the fundamental where Bm is required. To facilitate this, play B notes on the G row. Play this tune using only the fundamentals, as indicated: leave the chords out completely. It's a useful trick to have up your sleeve on occasions. In this tune long, fundamental drones are used to great effect.

D (D, F♯ and A) and Bm (B, D and F♯) are very similar chords and can often be interchangeable.

Tripping Upstairs

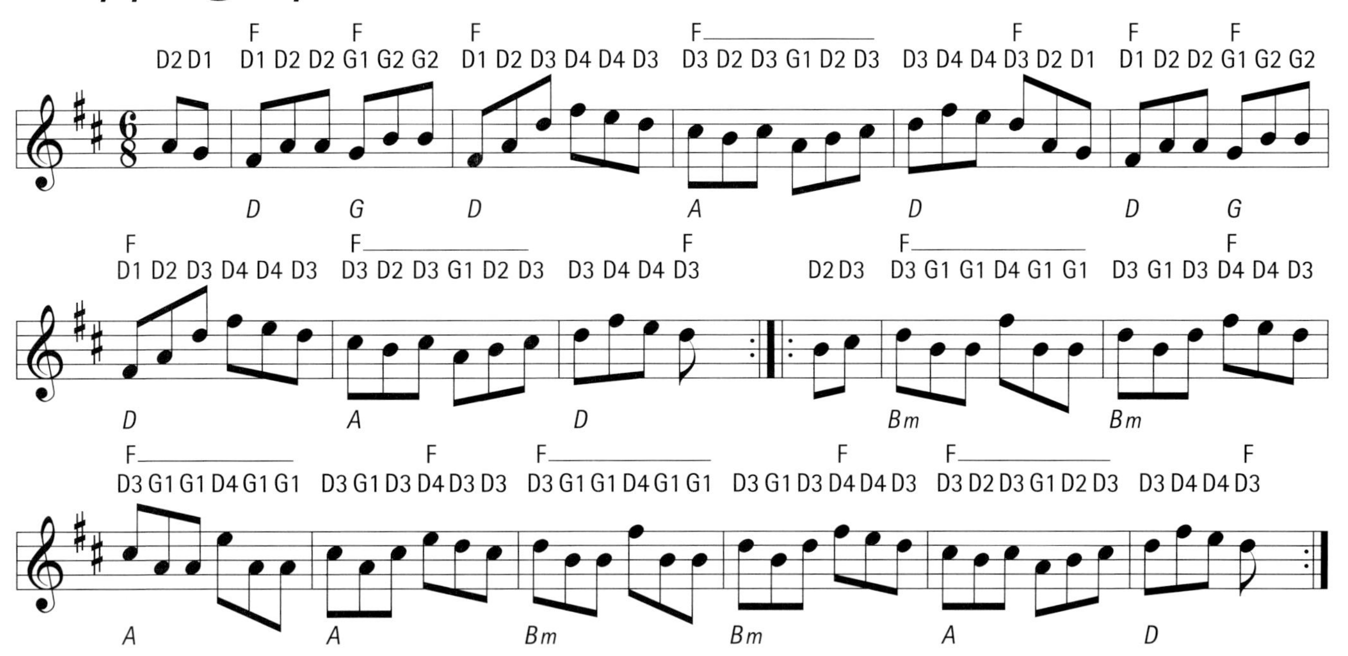

Slides and Slip Jigs

The Scattery Island Slide

On this page we have some slightly more unusual tunes, a slide and a slip jig. Slides come from County Kerry in the south west of Ireland and are written in 12/8 time. Slip jigs are in 9/8 time. These time signatures sound quite daunting, but you'll soon find out they're pretty straightforward.

Notice that a couple of new chords have cropped up here, A7 and D7. I've suggested these seventh chords purely and simply to bring up the subject. Often, in music books, the dominant chord (refer to page 22) will be the seventh, rather than the straight forward major. This is no obstacle to us, because a seventh chord is just the major chord with an added note, a flattened seventh. Therefore, when you see a seventh chord, say D7, simply play the D major basses. Problem solved.

Right! Let's have a look at the slide, *Scattery Island*. You're going to love this one: it's quite easy and sounds brilliant. Basically speaking, a slide is just a fast single jig: it has a rhythm somewhat akin to a hornpipe. The Um Cha Um Cha style of bass doesn't seem fit at all to slides. If you beat the bass in the manner of a jig, it's too much, but if you beat at half the pace, it's too sparse. So, we have to come up with something else. In *Scattery Island,* I recommend the fundamental only type bass. I've written it in above the fingering: have a listen to the soundtrack then give it a go. Note that some fundamentals are played quite quickly whilst others, where indicated, are droned.

On to *Drops of Brandy* in 9/8 time. It's no problem, it's simply jig time with each bar half as long again. Look at it another way: instead of beating the bass Um Cha Um Cha in each bar, you beat the bass Um Cha Um Cha Um Cha in each bar. Here's the last bar under the microscope.

Fit the normal bass style to this tune. I'm sure you'll find it dead simple: it fits so easily under the fingers, no shifts of hand position are required. *Drops of Brandy* crops up regularly in pub sessions, and is a great tune to use for that ever popular dance, *Strip the Willow*.

Drops of Brandy

The Key of A

Drops of Brandy

On now to something that many melodeon players never realise in a lifetime's playing. Not only is the key of A very much available for many tunes, it's also a really nice key to play in. It's exactly the same as playing in G on the B/C (the standard tuning in Ireland) box. The only difference being, D/G players are missing a note, the G♯ (equivalent to F♯ on the B/C box). Many tunes in the key of A don't contain the note G♯ and, in many of the tunes that do have it, you'll find, with a little manipulation, it's easily missed out. Irish polkas in A are great to play on the D/G melodeon.

Don't bother with playing the bass, leave it out. OK, you might be able to get in the odd tap here and there but, basically speaking, getting any reasonably continuous accompaniment is nigh on impossible. You might, using some very tricky cross fingering, get somewhere near on occasions, but you'll probably find yourself confronted with a rather annoying abundance of air.

For the final lesson here are three tunes in A: all are played entirely on the D row. You already have *Drops of Brandy* in your head, so this should get you off to a good start in getting to grips with this new key. It's relatively easy: all the notes fall directly under your four fingers: no hand position shifts are required. *Bill Sullivan's* and *Sweeney's* are two of the best Irish polkas around. Don't they sound great, and easy too? Again, no hand position shifts, except the small diversion in bar four of *Sweeney's*.

Yes! It's very nice to have the luxury of self accompaniment, thanks to our basses; but sometimes, it can be so refreshing to leave them out. Your music should sound nice, with or without the bass. Try all your repertoire without bass, make sure the bass is not disguising poor playing.

That's it! All that remains is for me to wish you well and remind you to practise. Good luck! See you at a session somewhere.

Bill Sullivan's Polka

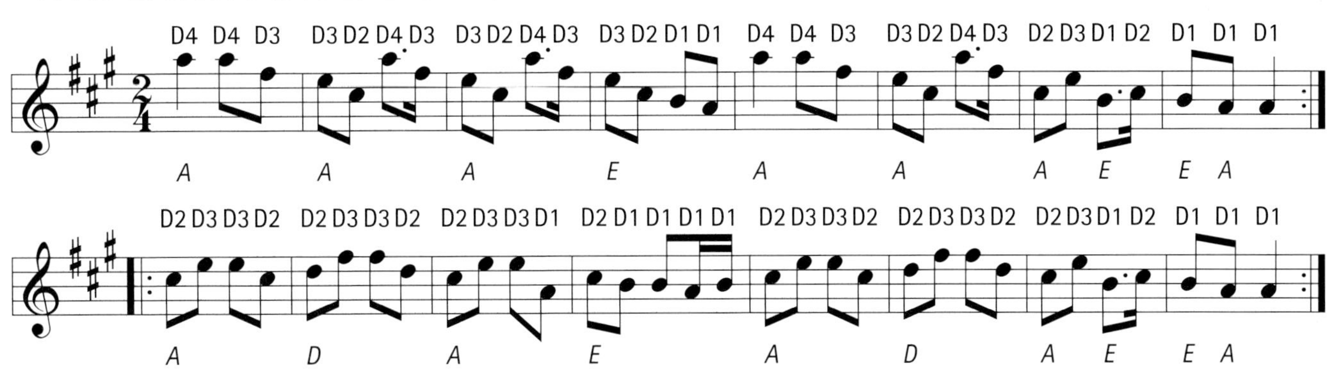

Sweeney's Polka

The Variable Buttons

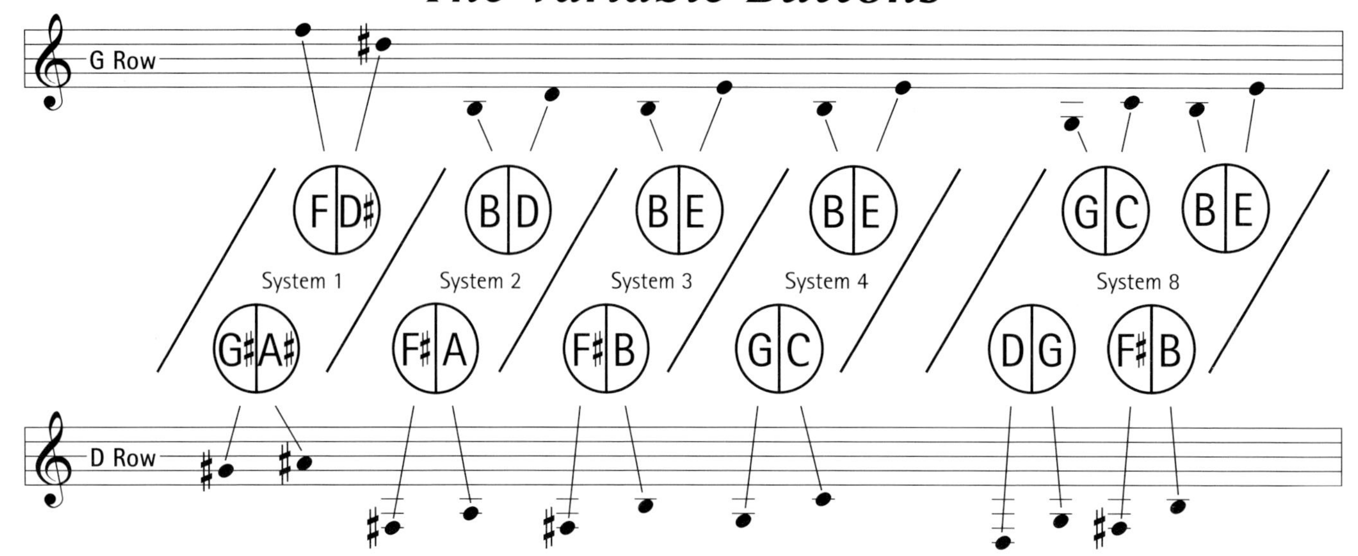

The variable buttons fall into two categories: accidentals, system 1 or low notes, systems 2, 3, 4 and 8. The above chart shows various options of what the variable notes are likely to be. Systems 1 to 4 will be found on third button doh instruments. System 1 has the greatest chance of being on your instrument, system 4 has the least. System 4 would be my personal choice.

Systems 5, 6 and 7 are found on fourth button doh instruments. They have both accidentals and low notes formed by combining systems 1 and 2, 1 and 3 and 1 and 4. System 8 consists solely of low notes. These are the notes I have on my personal fourth button doh instruments.

It's unlikely, but not impossible, that your melodeon has none of these systems.

Third button doh and fourth button doh are terms my colleagues and I use to describe melodeons with scales starting on the third and fourth button respectively.

Transposing

Because the melodeon can only be played in a very limited number of key signatures, you will probably find that from time to time, you need to do some transposing. Transposing simply means changing the pitch of a tune without changing anything else. With regard to the melodeon, for you to be able to read a piece of music, there should be one or two sharps in the key signature. On occasion three sharps will also be acceptable: the key of A.

The melodeon is a transposing instrument. Various pitches are available off the shelf or to order, for instance, D/G, G/C or C/F. Let's look at a fictional but extremely possible situation. You play in a trio: singer, guitarist and melodeon. The singer sings *Whiskey in the Jar* in the key of D, which you play along with happily, on the outside row of your D/G box. Unfortunately, the singer is a nurse, and because of her shifts, he can't make every gig. So, you have a stand-in available. The stand-in complains that D is too high for him to sing *Whiskey in the Jar*: he wants it in the key of C. No problem. Instead of choosing your D/G box, you pick up your C/F and play exactly the same as before and, hey presto, you're in the correct key.

OK! You can now select any key you want, simply by picking up a different instrument. It is important to understand that when you learn a tune in C on your C/F box (outside row), you still need to read it in the key of D. If you learn a tune in C on the G/C box, inside row, you will want to read it in the key of G. Learn to read music for the D/G system only: anything more will introduce confusion and is totally unnecessary. Whatever system you are playing, always transpose your music to D, G or occasionally A, to read it.

Transposing is simple, but take care when accidentals occur. What major key does the key signature represent? The chart below will tell you. Decide on the new key signature, D, G or A. Count the number of lines and spaces that the new key note is above or below the original key note and move every note this amount. For instance, to transpose from B♭ to G. B♭ is on the third line, G is on the second, so all notes need to be moved down two notches, one line ***and*** one space. To transpose from C to D. Move all the notes up one notch, one line ***or*** one space. Don't forget to alter the key signature to the new one.

Key Sig.	Key	New Key	New Key Sig.	Move
3 flats	E♭	D	2 sharps	down 1
2 flats	B♭	D	2 sharps	up 2
2 flats	B♭	G	1 sharp	down 2
2 flats	B♭	A	3 sharps	down 1
1 flat	F	G	1 sharp	up 1
1 flat	F	D	2 sharps	down 2
Nothing	C	D	2 sharps	up 1
3 sharps	A	G	1 sharp	down 1
4 sharps	E	D	2 sharps	down 1
4 sharps	E	G	1 sharp	up 2

It's safest to use the chromatic scale to transpose accidentals. Use the chart below. Let's say we want to transpose a B natural from the key of F to the key of G: it's two steps. So move the B two steps to C♯. Notice when you get to the end you start again at the beginning, making sure not to count the C twice.

C	C♯ D♭	D	D♯ E♭	E	F	F♯ G♭	G	G♯ A♭	A	A♯ B♭	B	C